"Dwight Gunter has written a masterful book with a sterling reminder that the church must submit to the lordship of Christ. With great eloquence, he points out that it's not *our* church—it's *his* church.

"His emphasis on the sanctified believer being the church to the world is a much-needed message.

"Every pastor and church leader should read *Seven Letters*. It has been written by a churchman who loves the church. I highly recommend this book."

—Dr. Stan Toler
Best-selling Author

"Pastor Dwight Gunter lives in the trenches where the church does its daily work. As pastor of an urban inner-city congregation, he understands where the rubber meets the road. Sadly, it is rare to have such solid theology and such radical identification with a hurting world show up in the same place. Gladly, it shows up in this book. Read this with an eye to the world around you and a deep appreciation for what the church is called to be and do."

—Dan Boone
President
Trevecca Nazarene University

SEVEN LETTERS TO SEVEN CHURCHES

Lessons from the Book of REVELATION

DWIGHT M. GUNTER II

BEACON HILL PRESS
OF KANSAS CITY

Copyright 2011 by Dwight M. Gunter II and
Beacon Hill Press of Kansas City

ISBN 978-0-8341-2607-7

Cover Design: Doug Bennett
Interior Design: Sharon Page

10 9 8 7 6 5 4 3 2 1

To Mom and Dad, along with my grandparents,
who modeled for me an active love for Jesus' church,
giving themselves up in service to him

CONTENTS

1
LETTERS
TO THE
CHURCH

Dear Jesus,

We have a problem in your church today. I've thought about it and thought about it. I've turned it over in my mind and my heart, and here's what I believe:

- Churches today don't know who they are.
- Churches today don't know what they're supposed to be doing.
- Churches today are trying anything and everything to be effective.
- Churches today are bewildered by worship styles and stymied by spectator syndrome.
- Churches today are confused by consumerism.

In the meantime, Lord, people are hungry for a relationship with a God who has substance, a God with character and integrity, and a God of grace. And they're having trouble finding such a God—finding you—in churches today.

Can you help us?

Sincerely,

Seeking You

I think that would be a letter people all across our country would write to Jesus today. I know some things about the church. I know, for example, that the church belongs to Jesus. He envisioned it. He instituted it. He developed it. And He planned it. It belongs to him.

So perhaps we write this letter to Jesus. And we listen for a response. We check the mailbox in our hearts and minds, and we look for a return letter from Jesus. Finally the response comes and he writes,

Dear Church,

Read my previous letters.

I wrote you earlier about these issues, and you can find the letters in the first three chapters of the book of Revelation. In fact, there are seven letters in those chapters. Read the letters.

Still seeking you,

Jesus

Jesus knew the problems of today's church before we did, and he wrote us letters in advance. All the letters have been applicable to all believers of every generation. And they are applicable to us today.

Churches today are building new facilities, expanding ministries, sacrificially giving monies, and sending people around the world on mission trips. Do these activities and goals flow from the heart of God and the mission of God in our world? Whenever we undertake any work in or through the church, we must make sure our foundation and focus are clear. We must make sure our mission and purpose are biblical.

It's fascinating to me that we always live in a state of transition, especially in the church. Don't you wish we could find one perfect formula and just do everything that one way and never have to change anything? Wouldn't that be easier? And wouldn't it be boring? See, we live in this state of transition because the world in which God has called us to minister is in a state of transition. The world God wants to love through us, the culture in which God has called us to spread the good news and to share the gospel of Jesus Christ, is always changing. And so we, as the church, are always adapting, changing, and working in a state of transition. It is vitally important that we routinely evaluate who we are *to be* and what we are *to do* as the people of God.

To discover God's answers to these questions, let's look at the letters to the churches in Revelation. And let's begin where John begins in chapter 1:

The revelation of Jesus Christ, which God gave him to show his servants what must soon take place. He made it known by sending his angel to his servant John, who testifies to everything he saw—that is, the word of God and the testimony of Jesus Christ. Blessed is the one who reads the words of this prophecy, and blessed are those who hear it and take to heart what is written in it, because the time is near.

John,

To the seven churches in the province of Asia:

Grace and peace to you from him who is, and who was, and who is to come, and from the seven spirits before his throne, and from Jesus Christ, who is the faithful witness, the firstborn from the dead, and the ruler of the kings of the earth. To him who loves us and has freed us from our sins by his blood, and has made us to be a kingdom and priests to serve his God and Father—to him be glory and power for ever and ever! Amen.

Look, he is coming with clouds, and every eye will see him, even those who pierced him; and all the peoples of the earth will mourn because of him. So shall! Amen.

"I am the Alpha and the Omega," says the Lord God, "who is, and who was, and who is to come, the Almighty." (Vv. 1-8)

Now when I have a letter addressed like that, where the sender says, "I am the Alpha and the Omega . . . who is, and who was, and who is to come," I want to say, "Okay, Almighty God, I want to take notice of this. What do you want to say to me here . . . now?"

11

The mission of the church is revealed in the beginning of the letter, right in the middle of this doxological greeting.

Now allow me to restate the problem: If we don't know who we are, then we don't know what we're to do. We'll try anything to be effective, which will result in all kinds of confusion. Feel familiar? Feel déjà vu-ish? Feel chronic?

So let's go back to the foundation in this doxology: Who are we, and what are we to do? Put your mind in reverse. I'm going to back into the answer. And I'm going to do so by stating first what we, the church, are *not*.

We are not a social club. Although building good relationships and living in community with each other is part of our mission, part of our purpose, and biblical, we are not a social club. Although we are called to bear "each other's burdens" and in so doing "fulfill the law of Christ" (Gal. 6:2), we are not called just to socialize. We thank God for the relationships we can form with other believers, for the sense of belonging we have among his people, and for the camaraderie that exists in the church wherever we go. But we are not a social club.

We are not a service club. Although we are to care for the needs of each other, to clothe the naked and feed the hungry, to tend the sick and help the helpless, and to visit the prisoner and house the homeless, we are not a service club. Although social justice is an objective of the church, there is a deeper calling for the people of God.

We are not a historical society. Although we have our traditions and creeds and build on the foundation that was laid by our spiritual ancestors, we are not first and foremost a historical society. Our view is not limited to the past. We may look back, we may learn from the past, and we may build upon it, but our focus is on the future. Where is God leading his people? We're not people of God who keep crying to go back into Egypt. Instead, we are longing for the Promised Land God has for us. So we are not a historical society.

We are not a sales organization. Although we want to introduce people to Jesus Christ, although we want to see the kingdom of God grow and increase, we are not "selling" a gospel or "closing deals" for Jesus. That's not our identity. That's not our main purpose.

So who are we and what *is* our purpose?

Our existence is "christocentric." That's a theological term for saying it's all about Christ. The church is Christ centered. Look at the phrases John uses in Rev. 1:4-5: the "grace and peace" is "from him who is, and who was, and who is to come and the seven spirits before his throne, and from Jesus Christ, who is the faithful witness, the firstborn from the dead, and the ruler of the kings of the earth. To him who loves us and has freed us from our sins by his blood . . ." Hear all those phrases that call attention to Christ? Jesus is the one who freed us. He is the one who made us. It was his idea.

The church is to be focused on Jesus Christ, to be centered on him. Our worship is to be directed toward him. Our energy is to be focused on him. The church is christocentric; it belongs to him. It's not *my* church; it's not *your* church. The church doesn't belong to a denomination. It is not limited to a theological system or a set of creeds. Jesus said to Peter, "I will build my church, and the gates of Hades will not overcome it" (Matt. 16:18). He didn't say he would build your church or my church. He said he would build *his* church.

This is not about buildings and facilities. This is about you and me, the community of faith, the church that's in existence if the buildings go away. It is this church that belongs to Jesus.

Our character is to be like Christ. Notice again what John says in Rev. 1:5: "Jesus Christ, who is the faithful witness, the firstborn from the dead, and the ruler of the kings of the earth. To him who loves us and has freed us from our sins by his blood . . ." Sin is first and foremost a *relational* issue. Christ freed us from our brokenness, from a strained relationship with our Creator, from that nonexistent relationship. Christ freed us from everything that had a grip on our lives. Christ freed us so that we could live in right relationship with him, so that we could be with him so much that his nature would rub off on us and we could be transformed into being more like him. Our character is to be like Christ.

He has made us to be a kingdom. We are a different culture from the rest of the world, with a different way of living and different values and ethics. We are the kingdom of the living, the kingdom of the free. We are his kingdom. That's why John said, "You, dear children, are from God and have overcome them [the world], because the one who is in you is greater than the one who is in the world. They are from the world and therefore speak from the viewpoint of the world, and the world listens to them. We are from God" (1 John 4:4-6).

That's why, when Christ stood before Pilate and Pilate asked, "So you're a king?" Jesus said, "Yes, but My kingdom is not of this world. My kingdom is not *like* this world. My kingdom is very different" (John 18:33, 36, author's paraphrase). Jesus meant that the culture of the church is different from the culture of the world. We don't operate by the same values, have the same ethics, or live the same way. We have a different set of standards and beliefs and code of conduct. That's why Paul said, "Do not conform any longer to the pattern of the world, but be transformed by the renewing of your mind. Then you will be able to test and approve what God's will is—his good, pleasing and perfect will" (Rom. 12:2).

The church's purpose is not about conforming to the ethics of the world's kingdom. Instead, it's about conforming to Jesus Christ himself—being "transformed by the renewing of [our] mind[s]."

So, *who* we are is a kingdom. We have different values from the rest of the world, and our character is to be like that of Christ.

Our mission is to be his priests. Look at Rev. 1:5-6: "To him who . . . has made us to be a kingdom and priests to serve his God and Father—to him be glory and power for ever and ever! Amen." This verse refers to *what* we do. A priest represents the people to God and represents God to the people. In other words, a priest goes before God on behalf of people and goes before people on behalf of God. He connects people and God. That is his role. That definition actually crosses the lines of different religions; it's sort of the universal role of a priest. It was true in Judaism, and it is true in Christianity. Since we, as the church, are now priests, we are to connect God and people. We're to bring God and people together for the opportunity of having a restored relationship. That's why Paul wrote in 2 Cor. 5:18-20,

All this is from God, who reconciled us to himself through Christ and gave us the ministry of reconciliation: that God was reconciling the world to himself in Christ, not counting men's sins against them. And he has committed to us the message of reconciliation. We are therefore Christ's ambassadors, as though God were making his appeal through us. We implore you on Christ's behalf: Be reconciled to God.

You and I—the church—are priests. Our function individually and collectively is to be priests. We are to *reconcile* people to God. We are to bring people to God as if God is actually making his appeal to people through you and me—together.

And isn't that exactly what he's doing? As our character, both individually and collectively, becomes more and more like

Christ, as our lives are filled with his Holy Spirit, he makes his appeal through us to the world around us. God's Word is proven true—that we truly are priests in this world.

But there is another function for a priest. A priest is also to make *sacrifices* for the sins of the people. Through these sacrifices, the priest is in a very real sense moving beyond atonement for sin into the realm of holiness. The priest is sanctified—sanctified holy and sanctified wholly. He is set apart for a particular purpose. He is to reflect accurately the character of God.

This concept became clear to me recently. I was thinking about our church in Nashville and the ministries taking place. I was contemplating what we're doing in our city and what God has called us to do. I was thanking God for the way our church is responding to God's call on us and how God is using the people of Trevecca Community Church. All of these things were flowing through my mind and heart as I was being interviewed by a reporter. He asked, "What do you see as the mission and purpose of the church?" As I began to talk about our mission, I summarized it by saying simply that we are called *to sanctify our culture.*

That idea may sound foreign to many Christians. Churches that emphasize being holy (Christlike) often think holiness (sanctification) means to withdraw from the culture. Believers tend to think sanctification requires living an isolated, "just me and Jesus" kind of existence. The logic is that if they withdraw from culture, they would not be tainted by the culture or by the world. They would not be *touched* by the sinfulness "out there."

So they withdraw and become some sort of modern-day monks or live a lifestyle holy and separate from the environment. They think that's what sanctification is about. But that's not what it's about at all.

Sanctification is all about *transformation*. These two terms are linked together over and over, not just theologically but biblically as well. Sanctification leads to transformation, but we are not transformed—sanctified—so that we can withdraw and establish some kind of holy club where we just hang out together and agree we are just so good and holy. Sadly, we have reached the place in many churches all across the world where we have forgotten many of the words of Christ. We remember some of them, like when he said, "[You're] not of the world" (John 17:16). But we have forgotten that Jesus then said, "[You are] *in* the world" (v. 11, emphasis added). In his prayer for his disciples, Jesus prayed, "My prayer is not that you take them out of the world but that you protect them from the evil one" (v. 15).

There is a power and a force, a Spirit God places in us that can withstand all of the temptation and the forces of the Evil One even as we are living in the middle of the kingdom of the Evil One. Jesus was saying, "Father, I'm not asking you to take them out of the world. I want to put them in the world, but I'm praying as I put them in the world, that you protect them from the Evil One. They are not of the world even as I'm not of it" (v. 15, author's paraphrase).

As followers of Christ, we have different ethics, different values, a different way of treating people than the rest of the world. We are to treat people with righteousness, love, and integrity—just as God does. Jesus says that his people "are not of the world, even as I am not of it. Sanctify them by the truth" (vv. 16-17). This is all one prayer. "As you sent me into the world, I have sent them into the world. For them I sanctify myself, that they too may be truly sanctified" (vv. 18-19). Jesus connected the concepts of *sanctification* and *going into the world for the purpose of transforming the world*. They are connected together in one prayer.

Do you know when he prayed this prayer? It was the night he was arrested, just before he was to be crucified. He said, "[This is] my prayer" (vv. 15, 20). In the moments when this Man knows he is about to die, don't you think he's going to get right to the heart of the matter? The heart of the matter, the point of his prayer, is, "God, Father, I have labored for three years with these believers, these disciples. They have become my disciples. You have given them to me. And now, just as you sent me into the world, I am sending them into the world. Don't take them out of the world; instead, protect them *in* the world. Don't remove them from the world; instead, fill them. Use them."

I believe God has called the church to sanctify our world, and the way we sanctify our world, the way we transform our world, is by *entering* the world. It's by visiting the jails, by entering the streets, by getting into the businesses, by becoming active in the neighborhoods.

When I was a teenager trying to figure out what I was supposed to do with my life, I shared with some older believers that I was considering being a politician. You should have seen their faces. They looked at me and said, "Son, you'll die and go to hell." That didn't make any sense to me then, and it still doesn't.

We need to get involved in the world because Jesus is involved in the world. It is our calling. If we want to sanctify our world, as we are called to do, we cannot live in isolation and think, "The world is just made up of *them*." We have to go into our world, just as Jesus did.

The Pharisees wouldn't believe in or follow Jesus. It wasn't because he had some crazy theology, for he always gave the right answers to their theological questions. Rather, they couldn't tolerate Jesus because they could not imagine a God in the flesh who would enter a sinful world to transform and sanctify that world.

Will the church today cease to follow Jesus because we can't tolerate a God who would enter a sinful world on a mission to transform it? Leonard Sweet in *SoulTsunami* said, "Can the church stop its puny, hack dreams of trying to 'make a difference in the world' and start dreaming God-sized dreams of making the world different?"[1] Neal Cole stated,

> The world is not very impressed with our sacred houses of worship; in fact, other religions have built more beautiful ones. We must let them see something they cannot reproduce: a new life in Christ. A transformed soul . . . now, that is something that the world cannot accomplish and is dying to see![2]

We can't transform anyone, but Christ can through us. We can't transform or sanctify the neighborhoods, the people, or our culture around us, but Christ can through us. The church will not transform the world—only Jesus Christ can. Going to church each Sunday will not transform lives—only the presence of Jesus in our gatherings and in our hearts can.

Jesus came in the flesh, and he still comes in the flesh. We, his followers, his disciples, are his flesh—his hands, his eyes, his feet, his mouth, his heart. We are the body of Christ. We are not divine, but the divine lives in us and through us. The purpose of the church is to do what Jesus did by the same power Jesus did it, that is, to introduce people to a transforming relationship with God the Father, Son, and Holy Spirit by the power of the Holy Spirit.

Those of us who have been set free and whose lives are being transformed and sanctified thank God he entered our world to free us and deliver us from a dying kingdom. We are members of a living kingdom, one that has a future. And we are now part of the priesthood that is given the mission to go back into the world.

So if you are discouraged and believe God is not miraculously working anymore, go to where God is really working. Enter the world of the broken and the bound, the hurting and the helpless. There you will see miracle after miracle. You will see lives that are being radically transformed, radically changed.

Dare to enter the world on a mission from God by the power of the Spirit. Someone may even say to you, "Because I saw *you*—how *you* were able to overcome, how *you* were set free, how *your* life was changed—I knew *my* life could be changed." You will want to cry out, "But it's not me. *I'm* not divine. Yet the divine lives *in* me and can live in you too. Therefore, your life can be changed too."

That's what the church is called to do. Our mission is to be his priests.

Our goal is to glorify God. That's what John says in Rev. 1:6: "[He] has made us to be a kingdom and priests to serve his God and Father—to him be glory and power for ever and ever! Amen."

"Glory"—that's a great word. When I learned in theology class years ago that glory is to be understood not just as praise, but as the presence and image of God, the entire concept was highlighted in my mind. The ramifications of glory understood this way are astounding. We come to Christ as we are, and his Spirit transforms us by his grace. We go into the world while we are still being transformed by the Holy Spirit working in us. Our character is becoming more and more Christlike—both collectively and individually. And now our mission, like Christ's, is to go into the world to seek and save the lost, heal the sick, bind wounds, work toward social justice, love the unlovable, include the excluded, and befriend, value, and recognize the marginalized and the disenfranchised.

As we enter the world, *the presence of God that is in us is then in the world.* You're in the world and the presence of God is in you, which then puts the presence of God in the world. His hands, his feet, his mouth, his eyes, his heart—all are in the world because *you're* in the world and he's in you. Then because he is in you and you are in the world, his image is seen in the world—that is, people see Jesus. They see God. They see the Father, the Son, and the Holy Spirit because he is living in you and you are where the people are.

We are infiltrating the kingdom of darkness. No wonder Jesus said, "The gates of hell shall not prevail against [you]" Matt. 16:18, KJV). We're going *through* the gates of hell. We're infiltrating the kingdom that did belong to Satan. It was his kingdom, it was of darkness, but now it's going to become the kingdom of light as we infiltrate it. This is what God has called us to do. In the process, we are being sanctified (transformed) and the world is being sanctified (transformed).

* * *

Our world is desperate for a relationship with God but not just for any god. Our world is hungry for a God with character and substance, integrity and grace. It's had enough of religion that kills in the name of God. It's looking for a God that brings life.

We write, "Dear Jesus, We have a problem in your church today." Jesus writes back, "Dear church, read the letters. Understand who you are, understand what I created you to be, understand why I have freed you and what I have formed you to be. Then do what you're supposed to do."

We are to be the church, the people of God, the kingdom and priests, for the purpose of sanctifying and transforming our world. This is done when his presence in us hits the streets around us.

Our world has had enough of would-be religions and also-ran faiths. Our world is frustrated with religions that aren't *real*.

Our world is exhausted with irrelevant churchianity. Our world is tired of Christianity with no Christ.

People in our world long to see what people have always craned their necks to see—God in the flesh—living out, enfleshing, and incarnating grace in the lives of people. Some people in our world today are like Zacchaeus, climbing up a tree just to get a glimpse of God in the flesh (see Luke 19). Some people are acting out in ways they never even thought possible. All they want is to see God alive and breathing, a God who is *real*. They're starving for that.

We can't just talk about it—we have to do it. We can't just aspire to it—we have to be it. We can't just wish for it—we have to live it.

Well-known theologian Frederick Buechner, author, professor, theologian, and evangelist, speaks for many people when he says, "For many years now I have taken to going to church less and less because I find so little there of what I hunger for. It is a sense of the presence of God that I hunger for."[3] And, it is the presence of God that our world hungers for.

"Dear Jesus, will you feed the hungry through us?"

Questions for Discussion and Reflection

1. What are some challenges the church is facing today locally? Globally? Other?

2. "The world God wants to love through us, the culture in which God has called us to spread the good news and to share the gospel of Jesus Christ, is always changing. And so we, as the church, are always adapting, changing, and working in a state of transition" (p. 10). In light of this quote, how has church changed in your life experiences? Are these changes good, bad . . . ?

3. The author identifies ways the church has misunderstood who it is and what it is to do. We have functioned at times as a social club, a service club, a historical society, and a sales organization (see pp. 12-13). Can you identify other ways the church has misunderstood its identity and mission?

4. How is the kingdom of Christ different from the kingdoms of this world?

5. How can we fulfill the mission of priests in this world? Is this mission to be fulfilled as individuals or as a community/ kingdom?

6. The author states, "Jesus connected the concepts of *sanctification* and *going into the world for the purpose of transforming the world*" (p. 17). Discuss the issue of the church "sanctifying" the world. How is this possible? How is it not?

7. What needs to be transformed in our world?

8. "We need to get involved in the world because Jesus is involved in the world" (p. 18). How can the church get involved in the world in order to transform the world?

2
FIRST LOVES AND DEAR JOHN LETTERS

Have you ever written a love letter? Have you ever received a love letter? Do you remember some of the ones you wrote as a kid? "Dear Jane, I like you very much. Do you like me? Check yes or no." I found out after a while that the best way get the reply I wanted was simply to write, "Check yes." Hey, it worked.

Well, sometimes.

What about Dear John letters? Those aren't so great, are they? You know, letters that say, "Good-bye," "Adios," "Sayonara," or "Go on—get on outta here" (for those of us in the South).

I had a girlfriend when I was in junior high school. We used to say we were "going together," so the opposite of that was "breaking up." She broke up with me six times. Six times! I suppose I'm a slow learner. Her mama liked me, her older sister liked me, but after six times, evidently she didn't like me.

In Rev. 2:1-7, we find a Dear John letter. Well, not exactly; it's actually Jesus writing a letter to a church who has by its very actions written him a Dear John letter, and so he replies:

To the angel of the church in Ephesus write:

These are the words of him who holds the seven stars in his right hand and walks among the seven golden lampstands: I know your deeds, your hard work and your perseverance. I know that you cannot tolerate wicked men, that you have tested those who claim to be apostles but are not, and have found them false. You have persevered and have endured hardships for my name, and have not grown weary.

Yet I hold this against you: You have forsaken your first love. Remember the height from which you have fallen! Repent and do the things you did at first. If you do not repent, I will come to you and remove your lampstand from its place. But you have this in your favor: You hate the practices of the Nicolaitans, which I also hate.

He who has an ear, let him hear what the Spirit says to the churches. To him who overcomes, I will give the right to eat from the tree of life, which is in the paradise of God.

I imagine John exiled on the Isle of Patmos. It's Sunday morning, the Lord's Day. He tells us he is "in the Spirit" (1:10). He is worshipping the Lord. He isn't letting his surroundings or his circumstances prevent him from worshipping Jesus. He has an encounter with the risen Lord, and Jesus begins to show him a revelation. This book is technically called "the revelation of Jesus Christ" (v. 1). John begins to see "what is now and what will take place later" (v. 19), and he writes it down.

It's interesting that the seven churches of Rev. 2–3 in Ephesus, Smyrna, Pergamum, Thyatira, Sardis, Philadelphia, and Laodicea were all located in that order along a Roman road. It was a Roman mail route, as a matter of fact, and as you read these chapters in Revelation, you'll find that the letters appear in exactly that order. You can see that Jesus is writing this letter through John to the church.

Think about it. Has it dawned on you that we are on Jesus' mail route? He knows our address. When the postman can't find us, when FedEx is fed up, and when UPS has passed our house, Jesus still knows exactly where we are. Aren't you glad? He knows what we face, he knows what we've done, he knows how we're doing, and he is sending us letters. We know them as his Word.

Jesus has a letter for us. Jesus has a word he wants to speak into the situations in which we find ourselves. And when Jesus speaks, life happens. Worlds are created. Oceans are formed. Foundations are stabilized. Stars are placed in their proper positions. Planets and moons jump into their correct orbits.

When Jesus speaks, life happens—the blind see, the lame run, the dumb talk, the deaf hear, the dead breathe air once again.

When Jesus speaks, life happens—the elderly receive hope, the children are blessed, the outcast find homes, the doubting grow in confidence, the disenfranchised find belonging.

When Jesus speaks, life happens—the possessed are redeemed, the sick are healed, relationships are restored, the sinful are graced with forgiveness, the bound are set free. *Life starts happening when Jesus speaks.*

If you read Rev. 1, you'll see God the Father, God the Son, and God the Holy Spirit—the Trinity itself—appearing on the day that is called the Lord's Day. John is "in the *Spirit* [Holy Spirit]" (v. 10, emphasis added). He sees the revelation of *Jesus* given to him by the *Father* (see v. 1).

So it's Jesus who is speaking, and each letter begins with a reminder of just who it is that is writing to the church.

This first letter to the church in Ephesus is no different: "These are the words of him who holds the seven stars in his right hand and walks among the seven golden lampstands" (2:1). Jesus has the authority to speak, and he begins in verse 2: "I know where you are" (author's paraphrase).

Jesus knew where the church at Ephesus was located geographically. He knew all about the city of Ephesus, one of the five greatest cities in the Roman Empire. It was a major commercial and trade center. It was not far from the coast and was where three major trade routes converged. Needless to say it became a very wealthy city. It was conferred the honor of a "free city" by the Roman government, which meant it was self-governing; its people lived by the Roman rule of law. It was a center of Roman justice.

Ephesus was also a center of idolatry. It had a temple that was one of the ancient wonders of the world, the temple for the worship of Diana, or Artemis. This temple was four times the size of the Parthenon in Athens. It was 425 feet long, 220 feet wide, and 60 feet high, with all of its columns overlaid with gold—an amazing piece of architecture.

Ephesus was a magnificent city. They had a highway seventy feet wide that ran from the harbor to the grand theater, lined with columns on both sides. The Great Theatre of Ephesus, located at the intersection of Harbor Street and Marble Road, had a seating capacity between twenty-five thousand and fifty thousand. The remains of the theater can be seen today.

Ephesus was an affluent and influential city. It was a cultural center and a center of immorality. And Jesus writes to the church in this fascinating place, "I know where you are."

After saying he knows where they are, Jesus commends them for what they have done well. You see, the church in Ephesus began with a great display of God's power. Paul had established the Ephesus Church in his second missionary journey. He had visited the church on his way from Corinth to Jerusalem and left behind some names you may recognize, like Priscilla and Aquila. When he returned on his third missionary journey, he stayed more than two years with them, so Paul spent about three years in Ephesus itself. In Acts 19 and 20, the writer tells us that God did extraordinary miracles through Paul and that the word of the Lord spread widely with great power. In fact, the church caused riots in the city simply because the power of God was displayed.

The church in Ephesus had strong leadership. Not only had Paul been there about three years, but also other pastors whose names you might recognize were there. For example, Timothy was a pastor at the church in Ephesus. He was pastoring there when Paul wrote to him the letters of 1 and 2 Timothy. Apollos was also a pastor in Ephesus. Even John himself—who is traditionally considered to be the author of Revelation, the gospel of

John, and the letters 1, 2, and 3 John—was also a pastor of the church in Ephesus. John was the man whom Jesus left to care for his mother, Mary, and legend tells us that John brought her to Ephesus and that she lived out her life and was finally buried there. This church had strong leadership.

This church had been effective in advancing the kingdom of God. As I said, its location gave it a great opportunity to spread the Word of God. People would come into town on business, and as they encountered Christians and heard about this new religion, this worship of Christ, Christianity spread. The church in Ephesus was responsible for starting other congregations throughout that part of the world.

The church in Ephesus was well organized. Paul, in his letter to the Ephesians, describes one of the best organizations of a church that we have to this day.

The church also had a global perspective. They weren't just wrapped up in themselves and their own surroundings. Instead, they would send money throughout the world, helping believers near and far. They had a global understanding of mission. In Rev. 2 the church is commended for who they were and what they did. In fact, in the very words of Christ, they worked hard, persevered, resisted sin, and critically examined the claims of false apostles. They were doctrinally sound, and they endured hardships without becoming weary. They were even involved in transforming the city. There had been a group of businessmen who had made a living using and abusing people, but the Ephesian Christians were so empowered by the Spirit that they disrupted the business by simply setting people free, by treating people properly (see Acts 19).

So as I mentioned earlier, a big riot ensued because people were set free and the church was at work. It was an incredible church. They were transforming their world. The church wasn't just making a difference in the world; it was making the world different. It was one of those churches that might make someone say, "If you're ever in Ephesus, you have to go to that Ephesus Community Church. I'm telling you, there is something going on in that church. A powerful God is at work there, and lives are being changed. You need to go to that church if you're ever in that part of the world."

Maybe I'm reading too much into it, but I think Jesus is speaking to this church now, in Rev. 2, with a tear in his divine eye, with the compassion of a broken heart. "You have written me a Dear John letter. 'You have forsaken your first love' (v. 4), abandoned it, cast it away as if it were nothing."

The words John is using here fascinate me. He says, "You have *forsaken* your first love" (v. 4, emphasis added). There was a point in time when you actually walked away. Yeah, your enthusiasm might have been growing dim, and it might have been fading out. You might have been losing your passion, and you might have been distracted or whatever. But there was a point in time when you could say, "I used to have this love and this passion, but now I don't have it anymore. I have forsaken my first love and walked away from it, abandoned it—my first, my foremost, my chief, my highest love.

Imagine that within the first fifty years of this church's existence, its people had Paul, Apollos, Timothy, John, and even Mary to mentor them. Having had all of these leaders, they still walked away. They forgot and forsook their first love.

Love is relational. It was their *relationship* with the risen Savior that was in trouble. It was their *relationship* with Jesus himself that was flawed, and they had lost their passion for Christ. They had work without worship, duty but no devotion. They had labor but no love.

When I look at this letter and wonder who Jesus is talking to in that church, I realize he's not talking to those who go down once a week or twice a week and engage in the immorality at the Temple of Artemis. He's not talking to those who are using and abusing people by their unfair business practices and mistreating people. He's not talking to people who don't understand the doctrine, who aren't doctrinally pure, who don't understand the worship of God the Father, Son, and Holy Spirit. He's not talking to those people. He's talking to the church—a good church with a great heritage, a miraculous beginning, and a track record of ministry effectiveness—but a church that had forsaken its first love.

How could that happen to them? How does that happen to us? It has happened to churches all across the country. When it happens to people individually, it happens to the entire church. So the question becomes, "How does this happen to us individually? How do we lose our first love?"

Maybe for some of these people in Ephesus, judgment took priority over Jesus. They were doctrinally pure. Maybe rules took precedence over relationship. They couldn't stay away from the "cultural temple" syndrome. Maybe their policy took primacy over people. Maybe ministry *for* Jesus replaced ministry *by* Jesus.

How does it happen to us? Maybe something comes along that looks better than the way of Christ—more money, a different job, a better position in life, or other attractive opportunities.

Maybe it's just plain busyness. Sometimes we get so busy—we may even say we're busy doing the things of God—but actually we're just plain *busy.* We are too busy to spend the time we used to in the presence of God. We know we're always in the presence of God, because he'll never leave us or forsake us, but there's something about intentionally spending time focusing on the presence of God. God is with us, but we need to listen to him and spend time letting him transform us and renew us. Maybe we reach the place where we decide we're just too busy for all of that.

Maybe we make excuses for sin within our lives instead of submitting it to God. We rationalize a particular sin because we like it and we're "good" in all other ways.

Maybe we lose our first love because we try to compromise our commitment to Christ. We ignore something God wants us to do or some area of our life God wants to sort out. We push it to the side until our hearts, which should be filled with love for God, become cold and callous and we lose our first love. We have the "form of godliness" but no power (2 Tim. 3:5). We look religious but have no relationship with Christ.

Jesus warns the church of Ephesus in Rev. 2:5: "Remember the height from which you have fallen! Repent and do the things you did at first. If you do not repent, I will come to you and re-move your lampstand from its place."

Jesus gives a warning. He doesn't just say, "Well, these people messed up. Don't say anything to them; they're gone." That's not the way Jesus treats us. He doesn't treat us that way because he loves us. He has this passion for us. You and I are the direct objects of the love of Christ. He's not going to simply walk away from us. He's not going to say, "Listen I know you did this, so that's it. You're gone." Instead, he calls us back to himself. He says, "You're going down a road that is going to end in your death, in destruction. Don't go down that road. 'Remember the height from which you have fallen' (v. 5). Come back. Repent. Come back into this relationship. Remember your first love."

Jesus loves us. So he tells us we need to do three things. First, we need to remember. We need to remember what the passion was like when we first began to walk with Christ. We need to remember how it felt when we knew our sins had been forgiven, the guilt was gone, and the freedom was there. Do you remember that? Do you remember when you first realized that truth? I remember. I still see it in my mind's eye. As I was lying there in bed, I said, "Jesus, how can you forgive me?" And Jesus spoke grace into my life, and my life began. I remember what I felt like when I got up the next morning. So Jesus says, "Remember."

Second, we need to repent. Repentance begins with recognition—I need to recognize what is wrong. Then repentance calls for redirection—I begin to redirect my life away from those things that are destroying me. I redirect my life toward God, toward life, toward Jesus Christ. I reorient my life. I reprioritize. I stop living for myself. I stop seeking my own way. Instead I reorient my life around Jesus Christ and all he wants me to be and do.

Third, we need to respond. Jesus says, "Do the things you did at first" (v. 5). So what did the Ephesians do at first? Acts 19 tells us they were filled with the Holy Spirit; the power and purity of the Holy Spirit was within them. They were mission oriented, spreading the good news of grace through Jesus Christ. Healings were taking place. People were experiencing freedom from bondage and demon possession. *That's* what they did at first.

Jesus is saying to the church here in Revelation, "I want you to love me like you used to love me. I want you to seek my presence. I want you to worship me with all your heart. I want you to orient your life around me and believe I am helping you."

Has busyness stolen your passion for Jesus? Will you repent and change it?

Have you been making excuses for tolerating sin in your life? Will you repent and change it?

If you have not obeyed God in a particular area of your life, will you repent and respond?

Remember, repent, and respond—or to sum it all up, walk in obedience.

Jesus ends these letters with hope: "He who has an ear, let him hear what the Spirit says to the churches. [And for the Ephesians, he adds,] To him who overcomes, I will give the right to eat from the tree of life, which is in the paradise of God" (Rev. 2:7).

There is hope. Jesus offers hope to those who remember, repent, and respond. There is hope for the church and hope for us as individuals. We are not without hope as long as we're in a right relationship with Jesus Christ. He will give us the strength and the power to be who he wants us to be.

Is your relationship with Christ what it should be? Have you forsaken your passion for Jesus? Have you allowed busyness to interfere with your relationship with Christ? Have you tolerated sin or disobedience in your life?

Do you need to remember, repent, and respond? The Lord knows. He knows where you are, and he's saying, "Remember your first love." Is it Dear John or Dear Jesus?

Questions for Discussion and Reflection

1. What images, memories, or agonies come to your mind when you hear the words "Dear John"?

2. "Has it dawned on you that we are on Jesus' mail route? He knows our address. When the postman can't find us, when FedEx is fed up, and when UPS has passed our house, Jesus still knows exactly where we are" (p. 28). What does it mean to you to know that Jesus knows exactly where you are?

3. "Jesus has a letter for us. Jesus has a word he wants to speak into the situations in which we find ourselves. And when Jesus speaks, life happens" (p. 28). What are some ways you've seen "life happen" when Jesus speaks?

4. After assuring the church he knew where they were, Jesus commends them. What was the church "doing right"? For what areas would he commend your church?

5. "The church wasn't just making a difference in the world; it was making the world different" (pp. 31-32). How would you say "making a difference in the world" differs from "making the world different"?

6. Jesus says in this letter, "You have forsaken your first love." What does "forsaken" imply? What does he mean when he says "first" love?

7. "How could that happen to them [a good church]? How does that happen to us? It has happened to churches all across the country. When it happens to people individually, it happens to the entire church. So the question becomes, 'How does this happen to us individually? How do we lose our first love?'" (p. 33). Discuss your thoughts.

8. In this letter to Ephesus, the call is issued to return to our first love. It is a call to remember, repent, and respond. Discuss what these steps to returning involve in the life of a believer. In the life of a church.

9. Reflect on the author's questions on page 35:

   "Has busyness stolen your passion for Jesus? Will you repent and change it?"

"Have you been making excuses for tolerating sin in your life? Will you repent and change it?"

"If you have not obeyed God in a particular area of your life, will you repent and respond?"

3
BE
FAITHFUL

Don't you love receiving letters of encouragement?

I've gotten some really interesting comments and letters of encouragement in my lifetime. For example, a member of one of the congregations I pastored told me, "You're a good preacher. Not the best I've ever heard, but good." I've had people shake my hand and smile as they walked out and, all in the name of being a blessing, say, "At least you didn't preach too long." And I'll always love the comment of a little lady who came in from another state about every third or fourth week; she'd walk out, shake my hand, and say, "Pastor, your sermons have been getting better lately." I didn't know whether to say, "Thanks" or "What was wrong with the first batch you heard?" If you've been in leadership, there have probably been times when you, too, have received similar anonymous messages or letters of "encouragement."

But don't you love letters that are genuinely encouraging?

I often read from an old Bible, a Bible that was given to me when I graduated from seminary in 1984. I use that Bible because it was from my grandmother. She's no longer with us, but she gave me this Bible and she wrote a letter of encouragement in the front:

Congratulations upon your graduation from the seminary. I appreciate so much your love for God and willingness to answer the call. Preach the truth. Stay true. Never compromise. Love people. Do all you can to win the lost and encourage and love the saved. Always remember, the devil never leaves us alone. Glad we can be overcomers. Love you and your family. Will pray for you always. Remember me in your prayers.

Harold was a living letter of encouragement. I had the privilege of being his pastor for almost eight years. Every Sunday, Harold would walk up to me, put his arm around my shoulder, and say, "Pastor, you're doing a great job. God is blessing our church." We had just gone through a major relocation program, we were on a shoestring budget, and we didn't know how we were going get things done, and it seemed that just when I needed an encouraging word, Harold would show up. He was retired and would come by the church. It was as if the Holy Spirit sent him. He would read my face, see the worry and anxiety, and say, "Pastor, don't worry, God's in control. Look at how far he's brought us. Look at what's happened so far. Don't worry; it's all going to be okay." Harold wasn't wealthy. He couldn't just write me a check for a million dollars and fix everything. He, like all retirees, lived on a fixed income. But he really was a living letter of encouragement, and that was an enormous gift.

Encouragement letters are wonderful to receive. The church in Smyrna received an encouragement letter in Rev. 2:8-11. There is something interesting about this letter. If you read ahead to compare this letter to all the other letters, you will find that this is one of the only two letters in which Jesus did not reprimand the church about some issue. It's one of only two letters in which Jesus didn't say, "You're doing well, but I have this against you" (see vv. 4, 14, 20). Instead, this is a letter in which Jesus said, "I just want to encourage you."

Here's what the letter says:

To the angel of the church in Smyrna write:

These are the words of him who is the First and the Last, who died and came to life again. I know your afflictions and your poverty—yet you are rich! I know the slander of those who say they are Jews and are not, but are a synagogue of Satan. Do not be afraid of what you are about to suffer. I tell you, the devil will put some of you in prison to test you, and you will suffer persecution for ten days. Be faithful, even to the point of death, and I will give you the crown of life.

He who has an ear, let him hear what the Spirit says to the churches. He who overcomes will not be hurt at all by the second death. (Vv. 8-11)

Let me give you some background so you can begin to understand this encouragement letter Jesus has written to the church in Smyrna—and the encouragement letter Jesus has written to us today.

Smyrna was an interesting city. It was founded by the Greeks in about 1000 BC. It was conquered in 600 BC and was reduced to a collection of small villages for four hundred years. And then someone came in and rebuilt Smyrna and it became a great city. It's very name means "myrrh," which was a perfume used in embalming and in the anointing oil mentioned in the Old Testament. So myrrh was a component of the oil that symbolized the presence of the Holy Spirit.

However, the city of Smyrna was like Ephesus; it was fiercely loyal to Rome and engaged in emperor worship. It was a free city and had a large stadium and a magnificent public library. It claimed to be the birthplace of Homer (ca. eighth century BC), the legendary Greek poet who wrote the *Iliad* and the *Odyssey*. When this letter in Rev. 2 was written, Smyrna had many different temples, including temples to Zeus, Apollo, and Aphrodite. It also had a large Jewish population, which was very hostile to Christians.

Smyrna was a wealthy and free city; it was a city of great importance, with a long tradition and with temples built to all of those Greek gods. It was a religious city; but it wasn't a *Christian* city. In that context, it was a city that made living a Christian life very difficult. In fact, there was an incredible persecution of Christians in that day.

Now, look at what Jesus says in the letter: "I know your afflictions" (v. 9). The word "affliction" means "to be under pressure, as in a heavy weight."[4] It is a sense of oppression, a sense that something is weighing you down, that you can't break free of it. It's something that grips you with its stress and anxiety.

Do you know what affliction is personally? Do you live with affliction at times, that weight that just seems to hold you down until you feel you can't breathe, as though you're just being crushed to death? Jesus says, "I know your afflictions." He says, "I know . . . your poverty" (v. 9).

There were two traditional words for poverty. One meant you just weren't very rich, that you had enough to survive and maybe enough for a few extras, but you didn't have any of the real luxuries of life. You'd say, "Well, I'm not very rich; I'm poor—in poverty." The other word meant complete destitution, not even two nickels to rub together. The word used in these verses is the word for complete destitution.

Historians teach us that the Christians in Smyrna during this time were persecuted until they ended up in poverty. No one would do business with them. They wouldn't give the Christians a chance. It wasn't that the Christians were bad or dishonest people; in fact, they were great people. But because they didn't conform to the culture and worship of the day, because they had a different ethical standard, because they lived differently, they were discriminated against and ended up losing almost everything.

So in Jesus' letter he says, "I know your afflictions and your poverty" (v. 9). He speaks here of suffering and persecution, even death. What do we do when we face these issues? What do we do today when we are confronted with affliction, poverty, suffering, persecution, and even death?

We don't think about persecution and death too often in the United States. Even though we at times say Christians are discriminated against—and I believe there are times when we actually are in this nation—we do enjoy freedom of worship. The kind of persecution we face is simply a by-product of choosing the way of righteousness.

But did you know that throughout the world today, Christians are being persecuted more than at any other time in the history of Christianity? So this letter to a church in Smyrna is very applicable to Christians today—not only in the United States of America but around the world.

We all know what affliction is about. We may know what poverty is about. We know what it means to suffer and to have that sense of challenge and opposition in our lives. So what do we do when we face these things?

One option is to just quit—to just say, "I'm not going to do this anymore. I give up." Many people have chosen this option; they decided that living a Christian life is just too hard, and so they write their letters of resignation. Actually, that's not a bad choice *if* we quit trying to do it on our own and start allowing the Holy Spirit to do it through us. But that's not the kind of quitting I'm talking about here. I'm talking about people who just turn their backs on Christ, who just walk away, who say, "No, tried that, been there, it's not for me. I'm moving on." And they may even justify it in the name of "the relative nature of truth today." So quitting is one option people have chosen.

Others compromise. They say, "No, I don't want to walk away from Christianity. I will accept that Jesus is Lord on Sunday and whenever I'm around Christians, but it's okay to live as if Caesar is lord the rest of the time." That has been a plague on Christianity for generations and generations. We decide to compromise because if we compromise our beliefs, ethics, and commitment, then we can get along a little better with the world's culture. Have you chosen to compromise?

But Jesus offers a different way. He offers a different challenge. Look at verse 10: "Do not be afraid of what you are about to suffer. I tell you, the devil will put some of you in prison to test you, and you will suffer persecution for ten days." "Ten days" does not mean literally ten days; it means a period of time.

Then Jesus brings up the extent of our faithfulness. "Be faithful, even to the point of death" (v. 10). Faithful to the point of death is radical faithfulness. It is extreme commitment.

And so the challenge Jesus gives us as believers is very simple and to the point: "Be faithful: don't quit—don't deny your faith, don't walk away from your commitment, don't compromise your belief."

Be faithful in the world in which we live, whether we are in the biblical city of Smyrna or Smyrna, Tennessee, or Smyrna, Georgia. Wherever we are, be faithful. Be faithful to your family, to your church, and to your place of employment—be faithful in all the situations of life. And be faithful to your faith.

Now that sounds good, doesn't it? That sounds like a good place to say, "Amen. That's good. Let's wrap up this letter." But you can't stop there, because you have to ask the question, "How are we supposed to be faithful? It's hard to be faithful these days."

Why is faithfulness such a challenge for us? Maybe it's because we are creatures of comfort. How many of you want to go back to the days before air-conditioning? A few of us can remember those days, and I don't think we miss them. Most of us can only imagine life without air-conditioning. We're creatures of comfort.

I personally like my comforts. I have a particular chair in my house. It's my chair, and I like my chair. I remember when I bought it. It's made of leather, and from being in contact with it I discovered I was allergic to new leather. I couldn't sit in it for very long because my skin would break out with a red rash. I had to wait three years before I could sit in that chair. But that's my chair now—and I like my chair. It's comfortable. We are all creatures of comfort in one way or another.

So when our faith becomes a challenge and it's difficult to live it out, we naturally seek our level of comfort. We want to do away with what is hard and ease back into a life of ease. We really do prefer the easy way.

Faithfulness may be a challenge to us because we don't want to risk failure. We've tried, we've failed, and we don't want to fail again. Do you recall the feelings of shame and worthlessness that came with failure? We don't want to go there again, do we?

Maybe faithfulness is a challenge to us because we want to preserve ourselves. We have this self-preservation mode of operation, and we're not really willing to suffer "even to the point of death" (v. 10). We certainly don't want to lay down our lives.

It's difficult for some to be faithful in marriage. Maybe that's because marriage isn't easy or it can be uncomfortable at times or it calls for us to lay down our lives. It calls for us to be vulnerable.

Are these the reasons why it is such a challenge for us to be faithful to God? Faithfulness to God is not always easy, not always comfortable. Faithfulness to God calls for authenticity, openness, and vulnerability. We have to lay down our lives.

Faithfulness is fine when we're in the middle of celebration and when we're around believers. It's not a problem when everything is good and we're not facing obstacles. But it's a different matter when our health starts to fade or the family faces difficulties or we're left out because we have different ethical standards. So we have the option: Do we want to quit? Do we want to compromise?

Hear the word of the Lord: "Be faithful" (v. 10).

So what does faithfulness look like? I looked up synonyms for "faithful" and I found words such as "trustworthy," "dependable," "loyal," "true," "authentic," "devoted," "dedicated," and "committed." I began thinking about pictures of faithfulness. It's been my privilege over the years to pastor people that personified the word "faithful." They're always there. Not just "there" at church. They're faithful. Not just because they tithe. They're faithful. They have a relationship with God in which they walk in faithfulness. They remind me of Abraham, who didn't know what the end of the road would look like; all he knew was that he was on a journey with God, a journey of faithfulness.

As I considered these people, I began to see pictures of faithfulness. It looks like a person grappling with the Word of God and how it applies to his or her life. It looks like a person taking this Word seriously and not just dismissing it by saying, "Oh yeah, that's just the Bible and I read it today, so check it off my list." Reading the Word and then setting it aside is not enough. We must take the Word and allow it to speak to us and transform us. Faithfulness includes allowing the Holy Spirit through the Word to shape our lives, challenge our beliefs, address our habits and our actions, challenge our ethics, confront our way of thinking, tackle our attitudes, and shape our very lives. That's what faithfulness looks like.

Faithfulness doesn't look like flawlessness. Faithfulness is not having all the answers. Faithfulness says, "God, here I am. I walk in relationship with you. Take your Word and, by the power of the Holy Spirit, shape me and help me become what you want me to be." That's what faithfulness looks like.

Faithfulness also means staying on that journey. Faithfulness is not a one-time event. It is a lifestyle. Living a life of faithfulness means we are continually shaped, challenged, confronted, and transformed by the Word of God. That's what faithfulness looks like.

Faithfulness means having integrity and authenticity, not just in one situation, but continually—living a life of faithfulness. That's what faithfulness looks like.

And so Jesus' word to the church in Smyrna was, "Be faithful. You're about to suffer persecution. It's been hard. It's going to get harder. It's been difficult. It's going to get even more difficult" (see v. 10). Now don't miss the fine print: "I just want to encourage you today. It's been tough. It's going to get tougher, but be faithful. And when, because of your faith, you are denied something to which you have a human right, be faithful anyway. And when your health suffers and things don't turn out like you hoped, be faithful." That's what it looks like; that's our calling.

But *how* can we be faithful? Well, in this letter to Smyrna Jesus shows us ways we can be faithful. First of all, we must not deny reality. Jesus did not deny reality. He gave the church in Smyrna a realistic picture. He said, "Yeah, it's tough. It's going to get tougher." But then he says, "See past the fear. Don't be afraid." Jesus understands our fear. It's amazing how many times in the Bible God or his angel makes an appearance and says almost immediately, "Don't be afraid" (e.g., Luke 1:30).

We live in a world filled with fear. Look at the news. Hear the stories of violence and tragedy. We can easily and justifiably live in fear.

We want to say, "What are we supposed to do, be faithful in the midst of fear?" And Jesus says, "Yes." But he doesn't say, "Look at the fear, and stop the fear." He says, "See past the fear." When we look past the fear, what are we supposed to see? We see God, because we are to remember who God is.

Notice that Jesus signs his letter to Smyrna at the beginning. He says, "I am 'the First and the Last.' I am there before you and I'll be there when we're gone. And I am the one 'who died and came to life again'" (see Rev. 2:8). In other words, death—the seeming end of everything—has no power over him.

Remember who God is. Look past the source of your fear. Acknowledge what causes your fear, face it, and don't deny it, but look past it and remember who God is. Remember he alone is God; there are no others.

It is fascinating that twice in Revelation Jesus tells us not to be afraid: 1:17-18 and 2:10.

When I saw him, I fell at his feet as though dead. Then he placed his right hand on me and said: "Do not be afraid. I am the First and the Last. I am the Living One; I was dead, and behold I am alive for ever and ever! And I hold the keys of death and Hades. (1:17-18)

———

To the angel of the church in Smyrna write: These are the words of him who is the First and the Last, who died and came to life again. I know your afflictions and your pover-ty—yet you are rich! I know the slander of those who say they are Jews and are not, but are a synagogue of Satan. Do not be afraid of what you are about to suffer. I tell you, the devil will put some of you in prison to test you, and you will suffer persecution for ten days. Be faithful, even to the point of death, and I will give you the crown of life. (2:8-10)

Notice the similarities. In each case a reminder is associated with the encouragement not to be afraid—the reminder of who Jesus is. He doesn't just simply say, "Don't be afraid." He says, "Don't be afraid; remember who I am. Don't be afraid; remem-ber who is with you. Don't be afraid; remember I'm the first, I'm the last. I was dead, I faced all the world could throw at me, and I am alive again."

Remember, Jesus has been there. When you go through affliction, suffering, and difficult situations and challenges, you want to talk with someone who has been there. You want to talk to someone who can say, "Yeah, I know what that's like. I know what you're going through. I've been there." That is an identity with someone that is meaningful.

And here Jesus is reminding us of not only who he is but also what he himself had been through. "I have suffered. I have died. I not only have been to the point of death but also have laid down my life. I have taken the worst the enemy could throw at me and now I am alive." If we remember Jesus has been there, we can choose, by the grace of God, to rely on his Holy Spirit.

When you read the letters in Revelation, it's easy to skim past the last statements where Jesus says, "He who has an ear, let him hear what the Spirit says to the churches" (2:11). That wraps up every letter and it's easy to take it as if it's just another "have a great day, sincerely yours" ending. But this ending is important, so don't miss it.

With the words "hear what the Spirit says," the Holy Spirit calls us to be faithful. But what is really happening is that the Spirit is *speaking* faithfulness into our lives. He is saying, "Be faithful." What an incredibly powerful word for us. When God the Father, Son, and Holy Spirit begins to speak, worlds are created. And here is Jesus *speaking* faithfulness into us. He says, "Be faithful; rely on the power of the Holy Spirit."

It is only by the power of the Holy Spirit that we are going to be faithful. And anyone who has ever been truly faithful to God has done so only by God's power. There are no superhero Christians who by themselves have been faithful to God in the midst of persecution and suffering. The superhero Christians who rely on themselves simply don't exist—and they never have. It is by the power of the Holy Spirit that we are made faithful.

Are you facing afflictions? Are there things in your life that are just crushing down on you, weighing you down? Sometimes we run at such a pace that we don't stop and think about what's really going on. But when you stop and consider your life, do you find something that is just holding you down—the stress, the anxiety, the issues, the challenges? Jesus says, "I know where you are; I know what you're facing; I understand. I've been there. And I call you to be faithful even to the point of death" (see vv. 8-10). And then he says, "If you're faithful, I'll give you the crown of life" (see v. 10).

You've got to love this. Jesus writes, "I want to help you be faithful. In fact, the only way you're going to be faithful is by my Spirit. So I'm going to make you faithful. I'm going to enable you, I'm going to equip you, I'm going to do what needs to be done for you to be faithful. And then when you are faithful, I'm going to give you the crown of life. I'm going to reward you for letting me do something through you."

That's a pretty good deal, isn't it?

Just about now you may be thinking, *I'm facing some major issues in my life. I'm facing some phenomenal challenges.* Perhaps the challenges are connected with your job or with your family. Perhaps you're dealing with habits or other struggles in your life. The issues may be physical or relational. And you're thinking, *I'm facing these challenges and I feel like something is just weighing me down.*

Jesus understands. And he writes, "Be faithful." But he never expects you to be faithful on your own; he wants you to rely on the Holy Spirit. Through his Spirit, he will give you strength.

But then he adds something very important—don't miss this: "He who overcomes will not be hurt at all by the second death" (v. 11).

What is death? We think of death as the end, right? And second death is the end of the end, right? And here Jesus says that this second and so-called final end is not the end at all. In fact, you'll not be hurt at all by what is supposed to be truly the end. So *there is no end.* There is no end for you if you are faithful by the power of the Holy Spirit; life is yours.

So again, do not fear. Instead, hear the word of Lord: "Dear church, be faithful."

Questions for Discussion and Reflection

1. Think about the meaning of the word "encourage." The word actually means to "give somebody hope, confidence, or courage"—or "to motivate somebody to take a course of action or continue doing something."[5] Can you remember a time when you received a letter of encouragement at just the right moment? Have you known a "living letter"? When have you intentionally been an encouragement to someone? How does encouragement change things?

2. The author talks about the meaning of *afflictions.* "The word 'affliction' means 'to be under pressure, as in a heavy weight.'[6] It is a sense of oppression, a sense that something is weighing you down, that you can't break free of it. It's something that grips you with its stress and anxiety. Do you know what affliction is personally? Do you live with affliction at times, that weight that just seems to hold you down until you feel you can't breathe, as though you're just being crushed to death?" (pp. 43-44). What is afflicting your life today? How about in the life of the church?

3. Jesus also talks about knowing the poverty of the believers in Smyrna—and what led them there. What do we do today when we are confronted with affliction, poverty, suffering, persecution, and even death?

4. The author suggests that in these times some make the choice to quit and others, to compromise. Have you found it true that these are choices believers make?

5. Jesus gives us as believers a challenge that is very simple and to the point: "Be faithful: don't quit—don't deny your faith, don't walk away from your commitment, don't compromise your belief" (p. 46). Why is faithfulness a challenge for us?

6. Discuss what a picture of faithfulness is and what it is not. Have you known someone who "personifies" faithfulness?

7. How does fear impair faithfulness?

8. In this chapter the author refers to the Spirit *"speaking faith-fulness into our lives"* (p. 51). What do you think that means? Why is that essential to our understanding of *being* faithful?

4
GET OFF
THE
FENCE

There are all kinds of fences. There are fences that protect, fences that keep things out, and fences that keep things in. Some fences distinguish, separate, or delineate, as in one field from another, one pasture from another, one neighbor's yard from another. One old adage says that good fences make good neighbors.

I love farms. Farms come complete with fresh air, barns, horses, saddles, and fences. I love them. My wife and I live way out in the country, right beside a farm with cows. Every now and then the wind will change direction and the smell of cattle will just kind of flow across our porch. If you've been raised in the city, you're probably thinking, *Oh, no,* but I'm thinking, *Oh, yes!* I love farms. I love the fresh air, barns, horses, saddles—and fences.

When I was eight years old, growing up in Hartsville, South Carolina, there was a family who attended our church, and they had a farm. They would often invite me to go home with them on Sunday afternoon. We had long Sunday afternoons. Church got out at noon, and we reconvened at 7:00 p.m. I would go home with these friends and eat a meal—usually prepared with fresh vegetables right out of their garden—and then we would play.

This wonderful family had a niece and a nephew who lived just up the road. On one particular long Sunday afternoon, Candy and Andy (you can tell they were brother and sister) and I were playing. We couldn't ride horses that day, but there was the barn, the saddle—and the fence. It was a four-board fence with each board being about an inch wide on the top. So I got this bright idea: We can ride the fence! We grabbed the saddle and threw it over the fence, and I climbed up and threw my little eight-year-old leg over the saddle, but the momentum carried me over and off to the ground on the other side.

It's pretty embarrassing to be thrown by a fence. I've attended horse shows and rodeos, and I watched cowboys get thrown by bulls and by horses but never by a fence. A fence doesn't even move! How pitiful!

I said, "We have to do this again." I grabbed the saddle, threw it back up on the fence, climbed up those rails, threw my leg over, and . . . well, you know the rest—same song, second verse. I was thrown by the fence again! Now by this time, I was getting mad about it. I'm thinking, *I am going to ride this fence if it's the last thing I do.* And so I threw the saddle back up on the fence, I started my climb, and Candy looked at me—she was the oldest and wisest one among us—and she said, "Dwight, if you get back on that saddle, you're going to fall off again and break your arm."

Now let me punch the pause button right here for just a moment. I'll get back to the story in a bit.

Jesus wrote a letter to the church in Pergamum; we find it in Rev. 2:12-17. He addressed a problem similar to the one I was having that day on the farm. It's similar to the problem that many churches have today and that many believers have as well. Let's look at the letter just a moment and see if we can find the fences here:

To the angel of the church in Pergamum write:

These are the words of him who has the sharp, double-edged sword. I know where you live—where Satan has his throne. Yet you remain true to my name. You did not renounce your faith in me, even in the days of Antipas, my faithful witness, who was put to death in your city—where Satan lives.

Nevertheless, I have a few things against you: You have people there who hold to the teaching of Balaam, who taught Balak to entice the Israelites to sin by eating food sacrificed to idols and by committing sexual immorality. Likewise you also have those who hold to the teaching of the Nicolaitans.

Repent therefore! Otherwise, I will soon come to you and will fight against them with the sword of my mouth.

He who has an ear, let him hear what the Spirit says to the churches. To him who overcomes, I will give some of the hidden manna. I will also give him a white stone with a new name written on it, known only to him who receives it. (Vv. 12-17)

We can see that this letter is filled with symbolic language and metaphors. The people in Pergamum would have understood these references; they would have understood what Jesus was talking about as he sent this letter through his servant John. But for us to begin to understand it, we have to dig a little deeper into this passage and we need to understand the background of the city of Pergamum.

Pergamum was different from all the other cities in Revelation because it was a royal city. It had been the capital of that region of the world for over four hundred years. It sat on a cone-shaped hill about one thousand feet high. In fact, the very name "Pergamum" actually means "citadel," and some historians have called it the most distinguished city of Asia. It had a Greek culture and was known for two things. Like many other cities, it was known by its great number of temples. One significant temple was a temple to Zeus. It was a grand temple with a large statue, complete with an altar to Zeus in front of that statue. Many of the city's people worshipped Zeus. Pergamum was also the very first city to have a temple built specifically for Caesar Augustus. So the city was engaged in the worship of all kinds of false gods.

The other thing Pergamum was known for was its great library. The library contained over two hundred thousand volumes. It was an incredible library for that age in history. In fact, it was second only to the library in Alexandria, Egypt. One thing that made that library so special was that until it was constructed, all writing was done on papyrus made from reeds gathered along the Nile River. Egypt had a monopoly on papyrus. So the King of Pergamum decided to create this library and hire the head librarian from Egypt. The king of Egypt found out about it and put the head librarian in prison so that he couldn't leave Egypt and take the papyrus technology with him. These days we pay fifty-eight million dollars for football quarterbacks. Back then, they paid that much (or its equivalent) to librarians. So Pergamum decided, "Since we can't have papyrus, we'll have to do something else." They put their minds together and developed parchment. Parchment was invented in Pergamum. Our country's Declaration of Independence was written on parchment, so you can see how long this writing material was used and how important its development.

Now, this city was a royal city and an ancient city. And in this letter Jesus says, "I know where you live—where Satan has his throne" (v. 13). As Rome was Satan's throne in the West, Pergamum was Satan's throne in the East. It became a Roman city in the year 133 BC.

As we zoom in closer on the hilltop city, we can see the church. And here we see they have a problem. After Jesus commended them, he said, "Nevertheless, I have a few things against you" (v. 14).

Their problem was not unique to churches of their day or to individual believers of their day. It is a problem common to God's people all throughout history. In fact, it is problem that has been common to God's people ever since God first chose a people for himself.

The problem they had was not that of denying Christ. In fact, Jesus knew the conviction of their faith. He said, "You have remained true" (see v. 13). Jesus knew the courage of their faith. "'You did not renounce your faith,'" he said, "even in the face of persecution" (see v. 13). He knew the commitment of their faith, for Antipas, a member of that congregation, had been martyred. Legend tells us that Antipas was roasted to death in a hollowed-out brass bull. What a horrible way to die! And yet, even in the face of that persecution, they did not deny their faith.

But time went on and a problem developed. In this letter you can sense a feeling of warfare, of battle, of confrontation. "These are the words of him who has the sharp, double-edged sword" (v. 12). In this letter are images of battle, images of thrones and authority, images of swords. It gives the impression that there are two sides to this battle and that choices have to be made.

So what was the problem? Look at verses 14 and 15:

Nevertheless, I have a few things against you: You have people there who hold to the teaching of Balaam, who taught Balak to entice the Israelites to sin by eating food sacrificed to idols and by committing sexual immorality. Likewise you also have those who hold to the teaching of the Nicolaitans.

It's interesting that this story about Balaam is cited (from Num. 22-25; 31). Let's take a look at what it's about.

After the Israelites left Egypt on their way to the Promised Land with Moses as their leader, they were passing through several territories. One of the territories was the territory of Moab. The king of Moab was Balak, and Balak didn't want the Israelites coming through his territory. So to take care of the matter, Balak hired Balaam, a would-be prophet who was sort of a psychic, a palm reader—the kind of individual who hired his services out to the highest bidder.

Balak sent his princes and emissaries to Balaam and said, "I want you to come and stand on a high hill and I want you to pronounce a curse on the Israelites" (see Num. 22:5-6). At first Balaam refused, and then a little more money was offered. Balak said, "Don't worry, I'll pay you. I'll make it worth your time and effort" (see v. 37).

So Balaam went with the emissaries and cooperated with Balak. But every time Balaam tried to pronounce a curse, it turned into a blessing. Balak got really aggravated—"mad" would be a better word—at Balaam, and he said to Balaam, "Since you would not curse them, but bless them, I'm not going to pay you" (see 23:11).

So Balaam went back home and the people of Israel continued to march through the land of Moab. But Balaam wanted his money, so he devised a plan and went back to Balak and said, "You know, I was unable to curse them, but I can tell you what to do to stop them. If you will send the women of Moab who engage in temple prostitution, who lead others in the immoral worship of false gods, along with some of the businessmen of your culture down to the Israelites, you will entice them to engage in immoral practices without them denying their God. Then their own God will destroy them for disobeying him" (see 25:1-2; 31:16).

That's exactly what Balak did. Balaam's plan worked like a charm. And Balaam would have received a great amount of money—that is, if he had survived. But God punished the Israelites for their sin, and in the process, Balaam died; he was killed because God brought judgment.

So it's interesting that in this letter in Revelation, the church is reminded of that story. Couple that story with the next accusation God brings, "And you tolerate the Nicolaitans" (see Rev. 2:15). Satan had tried the frontal attack: "We'll take one of their leaders, one of their people, Antipas, and we'll kill him and then all the Christians will cower in fear." But they didn't cower in fear. So Satan decided he would pull out an old strategy—what we might call "an oldie but a goodie"—and he dressed it up and called it the philosophy of the Nicolaitans, which says in essence, "This is about business and culture. You can have your worship, but business and culture is another matter. And so if you're going to make a living in this city, you have to engage in the practices of our culture. You have to buy into our ethics—and that's okay because you don't have to deny your faith in Christ."

Satan doesn't push us to say, "Well, I'm not going to believe any longer that Jesus is the Son of God." Satan would be thrilled for us to say that, but he knows the chances of that happening are really slim. Yet he also knows he stands a good chance of getting us to think we can believe in Jesus Christ while engaging in the morality, ethics, and values of the surrounding culture and society. And that is exactly what the church in Pergamum was doing. In fact, there is a phrase for this: "They tried to straddle the fence."

Now that's an old expression, it's a country expression, and it's an expression that takes us back to my "fence straddling" story.

I was determined to ride that fence. So one more time I climbed up onto that fence and I threw my leg over the saddle, and guess what happened? I fell off and hurt my arm. I started crying, and I ran back to the house. I told our friend, Aunt Mildred, "I think I broke my arm." I took an aspirin and went to sleep, then went to church—we were expected to go to church, broken arms or not—slept through the service, went home, and told Mom, "My arm is hurting."

My dad said, "Oh, you'll be all right. You've got to be tough, Son."

So I got up the next morning and went to school (when your mom's a schoolteacher, you don't miss school). But at some point during the day the nurse called my dad and said, "You need to take Dwight to the doctor."

He did, and when my mom got home, I proudly displayed the cast on my broken arm.

We can be guilty of trying to straddle, or ride, the fence. We say, "Well, I'm not going to deny my faith in Christ. Of course

I believe Jesus is the Son of God. Of course I believe in God the Father, the Son, and the Holy Spirit. Of course I believe in what we affirm as our confession of faith. Of course I believe all of that." But then we buy into the ethics, values, attitudes, and habits of our culture. We're trying to ride the fence.

Riding the fence is an attempt to be in two places at once. It's an attempt to be two different people at the same time. We call that *hypocrisy.*

The church in Pergamum wanted Christianity without commitment. They wanted redemption without repentance, spirituality without sacrifice, deliverance without determination. They wanted rewards without responsibility, and they wanted life without lordship. So they made Christianity conform to the culture instead of allowing Christ to transform the culture through them.

It's an age-old problem. Long ago when God called the Israelites to be his people, called them to be his witnesses to the nations, they tried to straddle the fence. They would worship God on the Sabbath and then bow at the shrines of the false gods during the week, because what happened during the week was a matter of business and culture.

But Jesus' message amid all this—the message he sent to the church in Pergamum and is sending to us—is, "Stop straddling the fence. Don't straddle the fence in your habits, in your attitudes, in your thoughts, in your values, or in your ethics. Get off the fence."

And to this message Jesus adds, "If you try to straddle the fence, you're going to be thrown. There is no way you can straddle the fence without falling off on one side or the other. You need to get off it."

So Jesus sends this word of warning in verse 16: "Repent therefore! Otherwise, I will soon come to you and will fight against them with the sword of my mouth." Fight against whom?

The enemy of the church, or those in the church who are trying to straddle the fence?

Notice which sword he is going to use. John picks up on this theme later in Rev. 19, when he says, "Out of his mouth comes a sharp sword with which to strike down the nations" (v. 15). Remember how God created the earth? He *spoke* the worlds into existence. As I mentioned in the last chapter about the letter to Smyrna, Jesus *speaks* faithfulness into us. And now Jesus says to the church in Pergamum, in essence, "I will 'take the sword of my mouth'"—a symbol of his authority and power—"and I will bring judgment upon you, for you cannot live in both fields at the same time" (see 2:16).

We have to make our choice. And what is that choice? Jesus said it in verse 16: "Repent."

Repentance involves *recognition*. The Holy Spirit says to us, "Look at what is going on in your heart and in your life. Look at yourself; look at your life." Recognition is needed.

And not only is repentance about recognition, but it is also about *redirection*. We must get off the fence and choose a direction to go. And repentance always means choosing God's direction.

Besides recognition and redirection, there is also *reorientation*, which means we are going to build our lives now around what God identifies as most important—what God says are the crucial elements of life. Therefore, we are going to build our lives around Jesus Christ himself. So Jesus says, "Repent. Recognize. Look at your life. See where you are. Choose a different direction. Reorient your life around Jesus Christ."

Then Jesus closes the letter with a word of hope, as he does in each of these letters. He says, "He who has an ear, let him hear what the Spirit says to the churches. To him who overcomes, I will give some of the hidden manna" (v. 17). That's fascinating! Immediately the original readers would have remembered the story about being fed manna on the way from Egypt to the Promised Land (see Exod. 16). That is the manna God sent down—heaven's bread itself, fresh every morning. He said, "I will give you some of the hidden manna." This *manna* wasn't just a remembrance of the bread God gave while the Israelites were on their way; it was the Bread of Life itself, the manna Jesus referred to when he said, "I am the bread of life" (John 6:35). Jesus is saying, "I am going to give you myself. If you repent, if you change the direction you're going, if you recognize where you are and reorient your life around me, if you stop trying to ride the fence, I'm going to give you myself."

Next he says, "I will also give [you] a white stone with a new name written on it" (Rev. 2:17). This would not have been foreign at all to the people of Pergamum, for a little white stone was used as an admission ticket to banquets. Jesus is saying, in effect, "I'm going to give you a pass, an admission ticket, and you're going to be able to enter my banquet." And his banquet is filled with his presence.

So do you hear what Jesus is saying? He comes right back to it. He says if we will just stop riding the fence, then he will give us himself and his presence. That means that when we have to choose between this field and that field, Jesus will help us make the right choice. And when we make that choice, he is going to give us himself. No matter what the world wants to dish out to us, we're going to have the presence of Christ Jesus, and if we have the presence of Christ, we can do all things. We can become exactly what he wants us to become. We can break any habit and do anything we need to do. We can be free and able to accomplish any vision because God himself is the One who will do it.

There are all kinds of fences—fences that protect, fences that keep things out, fences that keep things in. But there is also a fence that distinguishes, that differentiates. It differentiates two arenas—two fields. Can you picture those fields? Can you see the fence right down the middle? If you will let your mind's eye wander a minute, you will notice in one field there is a big crowd—the world—and they seem to be having a great party. But if you look in the other field, you will see Jesus Christ. You will see people gathered around him, and a celebration going on in his presence. You will see people in that field who are filled with peace and joy, people who have fought the difficult battles of life. Those people are on a journey, but they're in the field that centers on Christ.

The world says, "Earn your worth." Christ says, "I am your worth."

The world says, "Carry your own anxieties." Christ says, "Cast all your anxieties on me."

The world says, "Save yourself." Christ says, "I'll save you."

The world says, "Be happy." Christ says, "Be holy."

The world says, "Live by your feelings." Christ says, "Live by your faith."

The world says, "Defend yourself." Christ says, "Deny yourself."

The world says, "Honor yourself." Christ says, "Humble yourself."

There is a fence down the middle, and the Word of God says to us, "Get off the fence. Choose my field, repent, and I will come and give you my very presence."

Questions for Discussion and Reflection

1. This letter uses warfare imagery. In what ways does the enemy attack the church? Families? Individuals?

2. Has the church succumbed to that attack by compromising its values in order to improve its standing in the world? If so, in what ways has the church attempted to "straddle the fence"?

3. Are there issues that some people have identified as compromises but are simply traditions?

4. Are there issues that some people have identified as "adaptations to a changing world" that might be more accurately identified as straddling the fence or a compromise of Christlike values?

5. How are we to know when we're compromising or when we are truly adapting in order to be missional?

6. If the church has compromised, what are we to do about it?

7. What does repentance look like in the life of the church as a community?

8. What does redirection imply for the church?

9. How can the church reorient its life around the mission of God in the world?

5

GIVE JEZEBEL A MESSAGE FROM ME

I like power. Don't you?

My first car was a '68 Camaro. It was awesome!

My second car was a Datsun B210. It went seventy miles an hour at top speed—downhill, that is, with a strong wind behind me and the air-conditioning off. You remember those little cars? Turning on the air conditioner was like throwing out a parachute. *Whoosh!* You'd stop on a dime and get nine cents change. But I'd drive down the road in that ugly little green Datsun B210. Those were the good old days! Now that Camaro, I really did think was a powerful car—after all, it had a 327 Chevy engine. I thought it was fast until a few years ago when I moved to Nashville and got to drive a race car at the Nashville Super Speedway. That car had 800 horsepower—*whew!* I went one hundred fifty miles an hour on the back straightaway. Man, oh man! I was living out my childhood dream.

I like power and I'm sure you do too.

Now don't get a holier-than-thou attitude. Of course you like power. I mean, would any of us want to go back to the days before electricity? Of course not. And electricity is all about *power.* Few of us can even remember what those days were like. I have no clue what that life was like then, but I certainly don't want to go back there. We like our power. We like our power mowers, our power tools, our power boats, and our power steering. And if you're too young to truly appreciate power steering, ask someone with gray hair what power steering really means.

Jesus wrote a letter to the church in Thyatira in Rev. 2:18-29. This letter deals with an issue that has plagued the church for years and years. Let me give you a portion of the context, the background, of the city of Thyatira.

Thyatira is the least known of all the cities, yet it received the longest letter in Revelation. Thyatira was about halfway between Pergamum and Sardis on the Roman mail route (see chap. 2). This city fascinates me because it was known for three characteristics. The first was military; it was a military city. It sat out in the open, not a very defensible city, and yet it was an important city because Caesar's elite guard was stationed in it. It was a city whose sole purpose, militarily speaking, was to slow down any enemy attacks and protect the cities of Pergamum and Sardis.

The second characteristic of Thyatira was industry; it was an industrial city. It had trade unions; there were trade unions or trade guilds everywhere in this city. If you were going to make a living in this city, you had to be a member of one of these trade unions. There were road makers, tent makers, tanners, weavers, potters, and carpenters. The city was especially known for its weaving and dyes. In fact, in the book of Acts, we hear about a woman by the name of Lydia who was from Thyatira. She was a businesswoman, and she sold cloth made with the famous purple dye from Thyatira (see Acts 16:14-15). The city was also known for producing a bronze armor used by the Roman armies. Thyatira was a very prosperous, industrial city.

Thyatira was also known as a religious city. Unlike the other cities we have examined, it didn't have the big, elaborate temples that were common to those cities, but every single trade union had its own patron god. Trade union members would meet together and have a party, a sort of worship experience, and during their partying and networking, they would worship their patron god. If you were going to earn a living in Thyatira, you would have to be a member of the trade union, and you would have to go to these worship experiences—these worship gatherings, these parties—and participate in the immorality that was taking place there and pay homage to the patron god. The only god that was commonly worshiped in Thyatira was the god Apollo, who in Greek mythology was the incarnate son of Zeus, the main god of Greek mythology.

Given that background of the city, let's take a look at this letter:

> To the angel of the church in Thyatira, write:
>
> These are the words of the Son of God, whose eyes are like blazing fire and whose feet are like burnished bronze. I know your deeds, your love and faith, your service and perseverance, and that you are now doing more than you did at first. (Rev. 2:18-19)

Before we proceed to the next part of the letter, notice the commendation. Jesus says, "I know the church. I know where you are and what you're facing. I know where you've been and what you've done. I know all there is to know about you." And then look at the commendation: "I know your deeds" (v. 19). The word "deeds" is used throughout the New Testament to describe good works. These are works the believers in Thyatira have done that reflect positively on the character of Jesus. We are to do good works so people see them and then glorify our Father in heaven. That is scriptural, and this church was living that out. They were doing good deeds and Jesus says, "I know what you've done; you've done some great things."

Jesus writes, "I see your love" (see v. 19). That indicates love in action and is again tied to good works. It's about looking around and saying, "I'm not doing this just to gain influence or power; instead I am doing this because God loves us, God loves me, he loves others, and he wants to love others through me, so I am going to work and serve others."

He writes about their faith. They believed the gospel of Jesus Christ. They had faith and it was solid.

He mentions the word "service" (v. 19). As it's used here, "service" literally means "ministry." A number of ministries were happening in the church of Thyatira, important works of service. Again, this is tied to the idea of deeds and good works. A theme begins to emerge, a theme of a church that believed in helping others—and not just every now and then or haphazardly. Instead, these church members persevered in this, they endured, even amid all the challenges and difficulties of their situation; they kept on doing good works for others and helping those in need.

And then Jesus says, "I know your progress. You're doing more now than you used to do" (see v. 19). So this was a good church.

But then he says this:

Nevertheless, I have this against you: You tolerate that woman Jezebel, who calls herself a prophetess. By her teaching she misleads my servants into sexual immorality and the eating of food sacrificed to idols. I have given her time to repent of her immorality, but she is unwilling. So I will cast her on a bed of suffering, and I will make those who commit adultery with her suffer intensely, unless they repent of her ways. I will strike her children dead. Then all the churches will know that I am he who searches hearts and minds, and I will repay each of you according to your deeds. Now I say to the rest of you in Thyatira, to you who do not hold to her teaching and have not learned Satan's so-called deep secrets (I will not impose any other burden on you): Only hold on to what you have until I come. (Vv. 20-25)

So what's the problem? The problem centers on this person that Jesus names—*Jezebel*. The problem was not that there were women in leadership or that there was a woman called a *prophetess*. There are plenty of examples in the New Testament and the Old Testament of women who are not only leaders in the church but also proclaim (preach) the Word of God. So we know that's not the issue. The problem is something else. To understand this problem, we have to understand more about Jezebel.

Are you familiar with the name Jezebel? The story of the woman with that name begins in 1 Kings 16. Jezebel was the daughter of the king of Tyre and Sidon, whose territory included all of Phoenicia, and Ahab was the king of Israel, the ten tribes in the north of what was once a united Israel. Judah consisted of two tribes in the south.

Ahab was insecure; he was worried about his kingdom. Ahab was especially concerned with his power or lack thereof, and he saw that there was a growing power in the north, a region called Syria, also known as Damascus. Ahab asked, "What can I do to secure my borders, to somehow bring security and power to my people and to myself?" So he entered into a covenant— in this case, a military and economic treaty—with the king of Phoenicia. To seal the deal, Ahab married the king's daughter Jezebel (see 1 Kings 16:31). Marrying for political power was common in those days, yet it was not acceptable to God because God always wanted his people to depend on him alone. Instead, in Ahab's own human weakness, he says, "I need to ensure my own security, so I need to marry Jezebel." And so he did.

Jezebel brought with her the prophets of the false god Baal. In fact, she regularly fed 450 prophets of Baal at her table. To make matters worse, following their marriage Jezebel systematically began to eliminate all of the prophets of God. She had a big showdown with Elijah—or rather, the prophets of Baal finally had their big showdown with the prophet of God (see 1 Kings 18).

In this great story, Elijah said, "Let's determine today who the real God is" (see vv. 21-24). Elijah had all the prophets of Baal meet him on the mountain, just Elijah and the 450 prophets of Baal. They set the terms of the prophetic duel, which involved sacrificing a bull and placing it on the altar. They agreed that "the god who answers by fire—he is God" (v. 24b). The prophets of Baal proceeded to beat themselves, cut themselves, scream, and yell all day long, and nothing happened.

Finally it was Elijah's turn, and he stepped up and told them, "Well, you know what? It's too easy to burn this bull as it is. Let's soak it in water" (see v. 33). He filled the altar up with water, soaked everything, because naturally fire was not going to ignite on water. Then he prayed a simple prayer, and *whoosh!* Fire came from God and burned up the sacrifice, the stones, the soil, and the water, and the people killed all 450 prophets of Baal. They knew who God was.

Jezebel was furious, and she began to hunt Elijah. Most Wanted posters were displayed all over Israel: "Wanted Dead or Alive: Elijah, the prophet."

Now Jezebel eventually met her demise. You see, Ahab (Jezebel's husband) wanted a vineyard owned by Naboth. Naboth evidently had the best vineyard anywhere around. But Naboth refused to sell; he didn't want to sell it to Ahab even though Ahab was the king. Naboth didn't want to give up his land; it was a gift from God. So Jezebel said to her husband, "Don't worry, Ahab. I'll take care of it." She then had Naboth murdered so Ahab could take the vineyard.

Because of this evil activity, Elijah prophesied that Jezebel would be killed and that the dogs would lick up her blood—kind of disgusting, but that's exactly what happened. She was thrown from the palace windows, she died, and the dogs came along and licked up her blood.

What's fascinating to me is that here in this letter to the church of Thyatira, Jesus would choose to use Jezebel as the metaphor for the problem. I mean, there were hundreds of people in the Old Testament he could have chosen, a lot of people he could have referred to and said, "You tolerate this person and this person's teaching, but this is what he or she is doing." He could have used hundreds of other people's names, but he chose Jezebel.

I think the real issue in this particular letter centers on the issue of *power*. Jezebel wanted power; Ahab wanted power—that's why he married Jezebel in the first place.

In the day the letter to Thyatira was written, an age filled with many different religions, gods, and prophets, religion held power. Everyone wanted that kind of power. Jesus chose the name of perhaps the most power-hungry person in the Old Testament as the metaphor for what was happening in the church.

Now look at the symbols of power in this particular letter. We know that the members of the church in Thyatira could see the elite military guard in the city; that was a symbol of power. There were trade unions in the city, and money represented power. The purple cloth of Thyatira brought power. You might say the people were "dressed for success." And then there were the religious ceremonies in which you had to participate if you wanted power and prestige. You had to pay homage to the false gods to build your network for success and power. There was even a sort of local hero named Tyrendus, whose image placed on coins depicted him seated on horseback (one symbol of power) and holding in one hand a battle ax and in the other a club (two more symbols of power). Everything in Thyatira centered on power.

There is clearly a connection between the name Jezebel and the lust for power. But Jesus also refers to symbols of power. Look at what he says when he introduces himself: "These are the words of the Son of God" (Rev. 2:18)—not Apollo, the son of Zeus, but the Son of God. That's an incredibly powerful phrase. His eyes are "like blazing fire . . . feet are like burnished bronze" (v. 18)—power symbols, images of power the people would understand. He even says in verse 21, "I have given her time." Who

77

among us can control time? Who among us can hold time in our hands? We cannot, but there is a God who can hold time in his hands. That is a statement of power.

God is controlling the events themselves; he holds the power of life and death: "I will strike her children dead" (v. 23a). It's as if everything that lives and breathes and moves does so at the will of the God who has written this letter.

He refers to the power of knowledge. He says, "I am he who searches hearts and minds" (v. 23b).

He refers to the power of judgment: "I will repay each of you according to your deeds" (v. 23c).

Contrast the power of God with the power of Jezebel. Her power was self-serving, get-it-at-all-costs, run-over-everyone-who-gets-in-your-way power. She was all about getting and keeping power.

But let's be honest with ourselves and ask, "What's wrong with power?" I like power. I liked the 327 Chevy engine under the hood of that Camaro. I didn't like that one cylinder under the hood of that Datsun—or however many cylinders were in that car.

Is there something inherently immoral about power? Jesus had power. Remember the story Mark tells us—actually, most of the Gospels tell us—about Jesus walking along with the crowd pressing in, on his way to help someone. As he was on his way, he stopped and said, "Who touched my clothes?" (Mark 5:30). He knew power had gone out from him. Jesus had power. In Luke 4:36, we're told, "All the people were amazed and said to each other, '. . . With authority and power he gives orders to evil spirits and they come out!'"

Is there anything wrong with power? Jesus wants us to have it. He called the twelve disciples together and gave them power and authority to drive out all demons and to cure diseases. He

said to his followers in Luke 10:19, "I have given you authority
. . . to overcome all the power of the enemy." Later, he said to
them, just before he ascended into heaven, "I am going to send
you what my Father has promised; but stay in the city until you
have been clothed with power from on high" (24:49). According
to Acts 1:8, Jesus also told them, "You will receive power when
the Holy Spirit comes on you."

You see, Jesus wants us to have power. Paul and the apostles
used the power that had been given to them. In fact, Paul wrote
to Timothy that in the last days there would be people with the
form of religion and "godliness but denying" the power that is
in Christ and in Christianity (2 Tim. 3:5). He wrote in his letter to the Romans, "I am not ashamed of the gospel, because it
is the power of God for the salvation of everyone who believes"
(Rom. 1:16a). He said to the church in Corinth, "For the kingdom of God is not a matter of talk but of power" (1 Cor. 4:20).
He also wrote to Timothy, his son in the faith, "God did not give
us a spirit of timidity, but a spirit of power, of love and of self-
discipline" (2 Tim. 1:7).

So the real issue is not about power itself but the *source* of
power as well as the *use* of power.

In this letter Jesus is talking to people who can misuse power
to abuse others, to advance themselves, to treat others as less
than valuable, or to treat others as commodities. The abuse of
power is the ethic of our world, but it is not the ethic of the kingdom of Christ. The abuse of power is the way of Jezebel, but it is
not the way of Jesus. It is the value of our culture, but it is not the
value of Christ's realm.

Jesus writes this letter to the church in Thyatira, so evidently
there was a very influential person in this church, a man or a
woman, who was abusing power. He refers to Jezebel, so everyone might assume it was a woman, but it might not have been. It

was a person of great influence, and this person was using power to gain more power, to control people's lives, to mistreat others, to abuse others, and to mislead others away from the real issue of Christ and Christianity.

What is fascinating is that when the Jewish Christians concluded that Gentiles could truly be Christian, they required the Gentiles to follow only two rules: (1) they had to abstain from food that had been offered to idols, and (2) they were not to commit sexual immorality. Those were the two rules. In other words, rule number one—"Love the Lord your God with all your heart and with all your soul and with all your mind and with all your strength" (Mark 12:30); worship the Lord your God and serve him only. Rule number two—"Love your neighbor as yourself" (v. 31). Those were the two rules—pure and simple, reflecting the heart of God. And someone was abusing power in the church to lead people away from the heart of God.

When I read this letter I think, *Wait a minute. Do we fall into that trap?* I've been a part of the church all my life. I have seen people inside and outside of the church abuse others through the misuse of power. Have you ever seen that? Have you seen people who somehow—maybe because of their standing or position—gain influence and start to influence others away from God?

Earlier we addressed the issue of whether there was anything wrong with power. Power itself is not inherently right or wrong. It is the mistreatment of other people that is the problem. When I read this letter I pray, "O God, help the church to not cater to those who would grab at the power of influence. Help me to never abuse any kind of power you might give me. Help all of us as teachers, as leaders, as your people who influence others throughout our family and workplace, to never misuse power but to treat people properly through the correct use of power." Do you ever find yourself wanting to pray that prayer?

Jesus then gives a word of warning. He says that there'll be a price to pay for the misuse of power. He doesn't end his letter with a warning, though; he gives us a word of hope in Rev. 2:25-29, and even the word of hope contains symbols of power:

Only hold on to what you have until I come. To him who overcomes and does my will to the end, I will give authority [hear the power word he uses here] over the nations—"He will rule them with an iron scepter; he will dash them into pieces like pottery"—just as I have received authority from my Father. I will also give him the morning star. He who has an ear, let him hear what the Spirit says to the churches.

Jesus wants to give us power, not to abuse others, but to free us. He wants to give us power, but he knows power can be a dangerous thing. Power must be used in the right ways—to set us free, to pronounce freedom for others, to live a holy life, to face the challenges of life, and to overcome all the issues that would come against us in this life. Jesus wants to give us power.

But beyond that he says, "I will also give him the morning star" (v. 28). John makes use of the term "morning star" and says that Jesus is the morning star. What Jesus is saying is, "You want power, *real* power. You don't have to go out and make all of these unholy alliances. You don't have to play the games of the culture. You don't have to create your own false security. You want power? I will give you power. Power comes from me. Seek me and you'll have power."

Do you want power to face the temptations that come your way? Seek Christ; *he* is the source of power. Do you want power to treat somebody well when he or she is treating you badly? Seek Christ. Christ is the source of power.

Do you have barriers to overcome? Are you trying to figure it out financially? Are you trying to make sense of it all? Are you trying to deal with life, trying to survive? Seek Jesus Christ. *He* has the power.

He says in this letter, "I will give [you] authority" (v. 26). That "authority" is the right to exercise power. Jesus is saying, "I'm giving you power because I'm giving you *myself* through the Holy Spirit. And I'm giving you the right to exercise that power."

When life gets difficult, we don't have to run and hide. We can use the power that God has given us. When we face those things that would tear our world apart, we don't have to go back to the old way of life. We don't have to worship all those other false gods that we try to build around us. We need to only seek Christ. Jesus gives us the power to face whatever we need to face.

Think about those things that are weighing you down, those challenges, those obstacles, those things that tempt you to look for human ways to secure your own borders. Give all of those things to God and say, "Lord, here are all of the areas in my life where I need power. And what I need is *you.*"

"He who has an ear, let him hear what the Spirit says to the churches" (v. 29).

Questions for Discussion and Reflection

1. What are the good deeds, ministries, love in action, of the local church to which you belong? What is the church doing currently to make this world different?

2. How has the church historically used its influence to make the world better?

3. Is there something inherently immoral with power? What good can power serve? What harm can people in power inflict?

4. Consider the statement "So the real issue is not about power itself but the *source* of power as well as the *use* of power" (p. 79). What are the sources of power in the church? What should be the sources of power?

5. "The abuse of power is the ethic of our world, but it is not the ethic of the kingdom of Christ" (p. 79). How has the church abused power?

6. How have people within the church used their own influence to gain power?

7. Can you give examples of how the abuse of power has divided the church? Created unholy tension?

8. The author points out that legitimate power for the Christian comes from the presence of Christ in our lives (see p. 82). How can we as individuals use the power that comes through Christ? As a church community?

9. Pray together, "O God, help the church to not cater to those who would grab at the power of influence. Help me to never abuse any kind of power you might give me. Help all of us as teachers, as leaders, as your people who influence others throughout our family and workplace, to never misuse power but to treat people properly through the correct use of power" (p. 80).

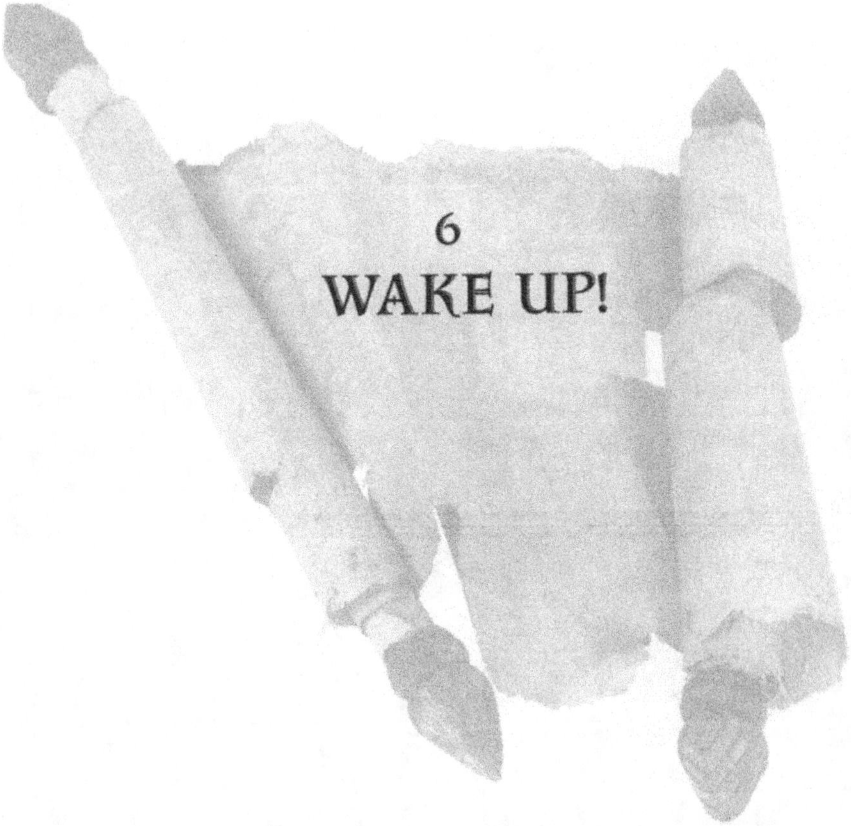

6
WAKE UP!

I love a good story. I particularly love westerns, especially westerns by Louis L'Amour. But some of my favorite stories are from Greek mythology, complete with chariots, swords and shields, hilltop cities, men and women of valor, heroes who find creative ways to do the impossible, and ships that sail into the unknown on the adventure of a lifetime. I love stories.

Such is the story found in Rev. 3:1-6. It is a story of epic proportions. The background story to this letter is also one of epic proportions. The city is perhaps my favorite of all the cities to whom these letters were sent, and the story of this city is my favorite of all the other city stories. It's the story of the city of Sardis, and this letter is to the church in that city:

To the angel of the church in Sardis write:

These are the words of him who holds the seven spirits of God and the seven stars. I know your deeds; you have a reputation of being alive, but you are dead. Wake up! Strengthen what remains and is about to die, for I have not found your deeds complete in the sight of my God. Remember, therefore, what you have received and heard; obey it, and repent. But if you do not wake up, I will come like a thief, and you will not know at what time I will come to you.

Yet you have a few people in Sardis who have not soiled their clothes. They will walk with me, dressed in white, for they are worthy. He who overcomes will, like them, be dressed in white. I will never blot out his name from the book of life, but will acknowledge his name before my Father and his angels. He who has an ear, let him hear what the Spirit says to the churches. (Vv. 1-6)

At the time of this letter Sardis was one of the greatest cities the world had ever known. It was built on a mountainous ridge about fifteen hundred feet high, overlooking the beautiful Hermus Valley. Sardis was perched on the end this ridge, which extended out from Mount Tmolus (named after the Greek god who judged the musical contests between Pan and Apollo) like a pier over the valley below. There was only one approach to that city, and that approach was very steep, narrow, and difficult. Sardis was virtually unconquerable—one way in, one way out—so it was easily guarded and very difficult to breach.

As the city of Sardis grew, it needed room to expand. The Hermus Valley at the foot of the ridge looked like the obvious place to build, so they expanded the city into the foothills, but the old city remained. It remained the citadel, the place that could not be defeated.

Through the new city of Sardis ran the Pactolus River, a river that was rich in gold. Thus the city of Sardis became very wealthy. In fact, the king of Lydia ruled from this great city; his throne was in the old city of Sardis high on the ridge.

One of Lydia's greatest kings was a king named Croesus. It was under Croesus that the city of Sardis and the kingdom of Lydia reached their pinnacle—and their ultimate defeat.

The abundance of gold in the area made Croesus a wealthy king. He was so wealthy that for centuries a person who was rich was said to be "as rich as Croesus."

Around the year 549 BC, historians tell us that Croesus was at war with Cyrus of Persia. Croesus had been defeated in battle on every front and had been driven back to his hilltop city of Sardis. Cyrus and the Persian army had surrounded the hilltop. Being the greatest army of that day, the Persian army assumed it would be able to conquer the city. Impossible! They attacked but could not find a way into the city to seize it. Time dragged on, and despite their best efforts, they could not defeat the city. Finally Cyrus, being a creative leader, said, "I'll give a great reward to anyone who can find a way into the hilltop city of Sardis."

Now we meet a man named Hyeroeades, a man who took up the challenge. As he watched one day, he saw a Sardian soldier drop his helmet over the wall by accident and then climb over the wall, scale down the mountain a short distance, pick up his helmet, and go back over the wall. So Hyeroeades thought to himself, *This must be the way.* So when nighttime came, he led a band of brave men up a narrow crack in the face of the mountain, and reaching the base of the city wall, they scaled it. On arriving at the top, they were astounded. They found the wall totally unguarded. The guards were all asleep, thinking themselves too safe to be on guard. And the city fell.

The hilltop city of Sardis was then forgotten for about three hundred years until a king by the name of Achaeus was fleeing for his life from Antiochus III, one of the generals of Alexander the Great. Achaeus remembered the old city of Sardis and to there he retreated. His troops were well supplied and found refuge in this unconquerable city. Antiochus III attacked the city and, like Cyrus before him, could not find a way in. Being a creative leader, Antiochus III promised a great reward to anyone who could find a way into the city. Now we meet a man named Lagoras who took up the challenge and searched and found a way—the same crack, the same fissure in the face of the mountain Hyeroeades had found centuries earlier.

Lagoras gathered a band of brave men, and when nighttime came, he and his men climbed up the narrow crack and scaled the wall. Upon arriving at the top of the wall, they, like Hyeroeades and his men long ago, found the wall totally unguarded. The guards were all asleep because they also thought themselves too safe to be on guard. And so the great, unconquerable city fell yet again.

Around the year AD 17, there was a great earthquake that destroyed much of that ancient city. But the city was so wealthy that when Emperor Tiberius said, "We'll send you money and funds to rebuild," the city responded, "No, we don't need your funds. We'll rebuild our city ourselves."

So if you walked into the city of Sardis on the day of the writing of this letter, you would find old, refurbished, beautiful buildings, hundreds of years old, interspersed with new beautiful structures—you would find a very wealthy city.

As you entered the gates of Sardis and began to look around, you would also find a degenerate, immoral, and corrupt city. You would notice the temple to Artemis, the god who supposedly had the ability to restore life to the dead. You would see other usual and beautiful Greek and Roman temples. You would also see the Jewish synagogue and other various structures typical for that time. And you would notice people who were engaged in the worship of Caesar, as wells as people whose worship of false gods involved sexual practices.

If you walked into the Christian church, whether it was in a home or in some other building, you would find people who were doing very well and were very comfortable. You would find people from different walks of life who were quite affluent because there was no pressure on the church from the surrounding society. The Romans left the Christians alone and let them worship their God. Christians didn't have to join any guilds as Christians in Thyatira did to do business. They could just live freely and make a comfortable living, worshipping as they pleased. They were free.

But there was a problem, and it's explained in the letter.

"These are the words of him who holds the seven spirits of God and the seven stars" (v. 1). Jesus tells the reader at the very beginning who the letter is from and by whose authority he is speaking. He is claiming his authority as the Son of God. He's claiming authority as the one who is seated at the right hand of the Father.

The next thing he says is, "I know your deeds" (v. 1). *I know.* The word "know" is in the present tense, and the statement is in the first person. That statement does not mean someone showed up at Jesus' doorstep and told him about what was happening in the church at Sardis. It means Jesus had intimate, firsthand knowledge of what was going on, not because somebody reported it to him, but because *he was there.* He was always with them. He knew what was going on in their lives. He knew the condition of their hearts, their souls, and their minds. He knew what was happening in their city. He knew what he wanted for them and from them, and he knew what was not happening. And so he says, "I know. I know your deeds, your efforts, your works."

What's fascinating about this letter is something *not* found in it. In almost all the other letters, Jesus commends the church for something, but here there is no commendation. You could point to his statement that not all of the people have fallen asleep (see v. 4) as being something positive, but that's about like saying, "Some of you aren't quite as bad as the rest." Not much of a commendation there. Jesus just gets right to the problem.

Two images define the problem. The first is the temple of Artemis. As I mentioned, Artemis was the god who, according to Greek mythology, was able to give life back to the dead. How appropriate that Jesus would tell those who were living in the shadow of the temple of Artemis that they were dead. He's pointing out the irony that those things around them which were supposedly giving them life were the very things killing them, the very signs they were dead. Jesus particularly and intentionally says, in effect, "You have the reputation of living the great life, but you are dead."

The second image Jesus uses is the city itself. I'm not certain if this church was located in the part of the extended city located in the valley or if it was part of the original city up on the ridge. But wherever the church was located, the members of that church would have known the history of their city. They would have recognized the meaning behind the words, "You are asleep" (see v. 1). They likely would have grown up visiting historical markers. They would have read, "This is the place where, in the year 549 BC, Hyeroeades led a small band up this crack in the mountain and over the wall to defeat this city. Here is the place where, in the year 219 BC, Lagoras repeated that same feat." They could do a walking tour of the old city and be reminded of the history.

Jesus says, "You're asleep. 'Wake up!'" (see vv. 1-2).

As you think about these two images—the temple of Artemis (the mythical god who was able to restore life) and the city's history (falling under attack while its guardians slept), consider them in the light of the letter's opening imagery in which Jesus proclaims his authority and authorship. Perhaps we can begin to get the point: *This church was spiritually dead; this church was spiritually asleep.* Jesus was writing, "I know your reputation. 'You have a reputation of being alive.' You have a reputation of being awake. 'But you are dead'; you are asleep" (see v. 1).

What an incredible indictment against the church. And the point is made even clearer with the use of the word "reputation," which is the translation of a Greek word meaning "name." In other words, your name might be Alive Christian Fellowship. It might be Awake Community Church. But in reality, it's a corpse; it's asleep.

Is this perhaps a problem in churches today? Is this a problem in Christianity? What does a sleeping church look like? What are the symptoms of spiritual sleep? How does it look when Christians drop their guard and drift off to sleep?

Maybe a sleeping church looks like it's just going through the motions. Maybe it has a "form of godliness" but no power

(2 Tim. 3:5). Maybe it looks alive, maybe it's loud, maybe it's energetic, but it's dead. It's not hard to drop our guard and go to sleep spiritually. So how does it happen?

If we don't spend intentional time focusing on the presence of God, spiritual sleep will come.

If we're not actively learning the Word of God and habitually studying the Word, getting into the Word and getting the Word of God into us, spiritual death is certain.

It is only by the Spirit of God working through the Word in our lives that we have strength. Otherwise our future will be filled with failure, spiritual sleep, and spiritual death.

If we find ourselves avoiding the weekly worship gatherings with members of the body of Christ, we will drop our guard and go to sleep spiritually. Our gathering to worship the Lord is a means of grace. It is God giving grace and strength to each of us that goes beyond anything I can do on my own. We find strength in our gathering. But when we fail to meet together regularly, we won't even think about sharing our faith with others (that won't even be on our radar screen). We will go to sleep spiritually.

And when we fall asleep spiritually, we find ourselves consistently justifying bad attitudes or bad habits. We compromise our ethics. We lower our standards. We accept a watered-down spiritual walk. Whenever the focus of our lives shifts from God to ourselves, we are going to sleep spiritually.

The danger of falling asleep is real not only for us as individuals but also for churches; it is true for entire congregations.

When churches begin to worship their own programs or priorities, they are spiritually dead.

When they're more concerned with their public image than they are with serving people, they are spiritually dead.

When churches love systems more than the Savior, they are spiritually dead.

When churches are more concerned with ritual than they are with righteousness, they are spiritually dead.

When people are more concerned with the law than they are with life, when they are more concerned with material things than they are with the spiritual things of God, then they are asleep spiritually.

It's a bit ironic that we live in a culture much like the culture of Sardis. We live in a culture that grabs all the pleasures of life it can get, but it is culture that is actually dead. We live in a culture that never sleeps, yet we're snoring spiritually. *Just because we're breathing doesn't mean we're living. Just because we're moving doesn't mean we're awake.*

During college, I traveled for a couple years with a good friend. We were in a band together, on the road performing in churches across the southeast portion of the United States. We usually stayed in the homes of church members and even in the same bedroom. Joe had a notorious way of appearing to be awake while he was asleep. In fact, he and I carried on full conversations he wouldn't even remember the next morning.

Once, in the middle of the night, Joe looked at me and said, "Cut it right here." I asked him where, and he said, "Right here." I asked him what he wanted me to cut, and he said, "Just cut it right here." I looked over and he was sitting up and pointing to a spot on the wall. He repeated, "Right here." I said, "Right there?" and he said, "Yeah, right there." I said, "All right. I just cut it." He said, "Thank you," and lay back down. I had never moved. That was neither the first nor the last such episode. My friend had nighttime conversations with doors, chairs, pillows— I loved it. It was fun; I never knew what to expect.

Just because you're moving doesn't mean you're awake. Churches often will go through the motions—the same routines they've followed for years—and they'll have a form of godliness and a reputation for being outstanding congregations. They'll tell themselves, "We had a great church service today because we sang three hymns and heard three points in a sermon and then we went home." But actually these churches are not awake. They're not living.

You may think that if we incorporate contemporary worship, we will wake up. Or if the pastor preaches loud and long, that will fix the problem. The truth is those can be just different modes of sleep.

What will wake us up and keep us awake and alert?

The answer is the Holy Spirit. The answer is people living their lives in concert with the mission of God.

The spiritual achievements we are able to accomplish as a church cannot be done by an individual or a group of individuals. God brings the church together for a mission, for a purpose. And when we focus on God's plan for the church and submit to the work of the Holy Spirit among us, things happen. The church wakes up. People move from death to life. Lives are transformed. People are set free spiritually. We are made over in the image of Christ because our focus is on God.

We hear in all of these letters the words of warning, the words of caution, words that say, "Don't go down that particular road, because if you do, it will result in tragedy or loss. Instead, wake up!"

So what do we do if we find ourselves spiritually sleeping? How do we wake up? Jesus tells us here in his letter.

The first thing we have to do is *recognize the problem*. These sentences are structured like short phrases. Musicians will understand if I refer to them as "staccato phrases"; they're short and to the point. The words are like light slaps on the face when you're trying to wake someone up and rouse him or her from sleep: "Wake up! Strengthen what remains and is about to die, for I have not found your deeds complete" (Rev. 3:2). So recognize the problem; wake up and determine what's wrong.

If you realize there may be a problem in your spiritual life, if you think you might be sleeping spiritually and want to begin the process of waking up, you need to get into the Word of God. Return to a focused time of praying and seeking God and listening to him. Ask the Holy Spirit to lead you and "restore what remains."

Next, *remember*. "Remember . . . what you have received" (v. 3)—the gift of Jesus Christ. And with Jesus Christ, what have we received? "My God will meet all your needs according to his glorious riches in Christ Jesus" (Phil. 4:19). We've received a whole storehouse of supplies for living our lives through Jesus Christ.

We've received freedom: "If the Son sets you free, you will be free indeed" (John 8:36).

We've received life: "I am come that they might have life, and that they might have it more abundantly" (John 10:10b, KJV). Not just somewhat, but *abundantly*—overflowing life.

I could go on and on listing what we have received in Jesus Christ, but what we have received more than anything else is *forgiveness of sins, a transformed heart, life everlasting,* and *the promise of the presence of God.* No matter where we go, what we do, what we face, what we encounter, or what challenges us in life, we have received Jesus himself. *"Remember . . .* what you have received" (Rev. 3:3, emphasis added).

Next, he says, *"Repent."* Repent of our lifelessness. Repent of our hypocritical lifestyles. Repent of our emphasis on reputation—having that "form of godliness" but not the power (2 Tim. 3:5).

Next, he says to *renew*. Renew the mission. Renewing the mission implies walking in obedience. "Remember, therefore, what you have received and heard; obey it" (Rev. 3:3). *Obey* it.

That means to guard it. That's an interesting word. That word describes what the guards were supposed to be doing on top of the wall when the enemy was scaling the mountain. That word says, "Keep an eye on this place. The enemy's come through here once before, and we don't want the enemy to come through here again. Keep your eyes open, guard this, obey this." That's why he's saying, "Obey." Take a lesson from history: obey. Take a look at it, guard your life, guard your heart and mind in Christ Jesus.

And finally, *release* the Holy Spirit to work in your life. "He who has an ear, let him hear what the Spirit says to the churches" (v. 6). You see, it is only by the Holy Spirit that a church can have the power to be awake and alive. What we need is the Holy Spirit. What we *must* have is the Holy Spirit. And so the church calls to him, "Holy Spirit, this is your home. Work in and among us—do what you need to do among us and in our own individual lives."

If we, as individuals, are to stay awake spiritually or if we are to wake up spiritually, we have to say, "Holy Spirit, I am not going to control my life anymore; instead, I give my life to you. I've been trying to control it, trying to deal with it, trying to handle it, but instead now I'm going to release it to you." Then we wake up spiritually.

He closes these instructions with a warning that again points back to Sardian history, reminding them, "If you don't wake up, you're going to fall. The enemy is going to slip in when you don't expect it, and you will be defeated. Keep an eye on the walls. Watch. Be on guard. Obey."

But before Jesus closes the letter, he gives hope. There was a remnant who was awake, fellowshipping and walking with Jesus. When he considers the remnant, he says, "There are some of you who aren't asleep, there are some of you who are not spiritually dead, and you're going to walk with me; you're going to live" (see vv. 4-5).

Imagine what might have happened if someone had decided to go for a walk on the night Hyeroeades was planning to bring his band of soldiers up the mountain and over the wall to attack the city? What if somebody was just out for a stroll, and after seeing what was going on, said, "Wait a minute—where are the guards? The guards are supposed to be on the walls of this city. We have an enemy at the doorstep. Where are the guards?" Can you imagine the reaction? People would go to the guardhouse, knock on the door, and scream, "Get up! Why are you asleep? There's an enemy at the gate! There's an enemy right now, wanting to defeat us. Get up and get to the wall. Pay attention to what's going on so that we're not destroyed. Wake up! Get to the wall!"

What would have happened if those guards had heeded that warning? What if they'd gotten up, gone to the wall, seen the enemy coming, and were ready to meet them?

That's what the Holy Spirit's doing in this letter. And maybe the Holy Spirit is walking to the door of your heart and saying, "You're supposed to be guarding this! You're supposed to be watching over this! Look at this area of your life, at this attitude in your life, at this habit in your life. You're supposed to be obeying me in this. Wake up! There is an enemy at the gate who is seeking to destroy you."

Wake up!

Questions for Discussion and Reflection

1. Jesus knows what is going on in your life. How does that encourage you? How does that make you uncomfortable?

2. What gives Jesus the right to confront us over issues in our lives?

3. In what ways can the church give the impression of life but be dead in reality?

4. When people are asleep, they are oblivious to what is happening around them. In what ways is the church asleep and thus unaware of surrounding events?

5. The author writes, "It's a bit ironic that we live in a culture much like the culture of Sardis. We live in a culture that grabs all the pleasures of life it can get, but it is culture that is actually dead. We live in a culture that never sleeps, yet we're snoring spiritually" (p. 94). What does a sleeping church look like? What are the symptoms of spiritual sleep? How does it look when Christians drop their guard and drift off to sleep? (see pp. 92-94).

6. How can the church wake up? What do we need to do to help wake the church up from spiritual slumber? Individually? Corporately?

7. What role does repentance play in bringing life to a dead church?

8. How can the church release the Holy Spirit to work freely among us?

7
CARPE DIEM

When I was twelve years old, my favorite swimming hole was a little four-acre pond in our neighborhood we called the lake. It looked huge to my younger brother and me. We loved that place. There was a section of the shoreline that formed a cliff. The cliff was only about fifteen feet high, but to a twelve-year-old it was intimidating. At the edge of the cliff the water was about three feet deep. But as soon as you moved four or five feet farther into the pond, the bottom dropped and the water was suddenly over your head. We learned that one of the most fun things to do was to back up, get a running start, and just leap off that cliff, hanging in the air for what seemed like forever before beginning our descent into the water. We thought, *Man, this is living; this is fun!* Every day we could, we would go to the lake. Mom's rule, to avoid tons of dirty laundry, was that we had to swim in the same pair of cutoff blue jeans every time we went on the same day. But as long as we followed the rules, we could go to the lake.

Just to the left of our jumping-off point on the cliff stood this tall Virginia pine. The first limb on the trunk was about twenty feet high. Someone, somehow, some years back had climbed the trunk of the pine and tied a big rope to the lowest large limb. The bigger kids would grab that rope and swing out off the cliff and drop into the water. I thought this was phenomenal, but I was too scared to do it. I stuck with the cliff; I was an expert at that—run, leap into the air, fall into the lake—nothing to it. I'd look down my nose at the little kids and say, "So are you scared to jump off the cliff?" And the teenagers would look down their noses at me and say, "Are you scared to swing off the rope?"

One day—I don't know what possessed me—I grabbed the rope and said, "I think I'll just swing out over the lake." One of my *friends* said, "I dare you. I double dare you!" Of course, any self-respecting twelve-year-old boy in Hartsville, South Carolina, is going to take a dare like that. So I grabbed the rope, backed up, and ran toward the cliff. Just as my feet left the ground and I was suspended there in the air over the lake, my *friend* yelled, "Chicken if you don't drop!" Of course, any self-respecting twelve-year-old boy in Hartsville, South Carolina, is not going to allow himself to be called chicken.

So I let go of the rope. My stomach went to my throat, and—*splash!*—I began to fight my way back up through the water. I took my first breath of air, and then I couldn't wait until I could get up there and grab that rope again!

Without even realizing it, when my *friend* Scotty yelled at me, he had thrown down a challenge. And I've discovered I love a challenge. When somebody says it can't be done, I love to be part of the team that does it.

So what is a challenge? A challenge is an opportunity dressed up most of the time in hard, uncomfortable work clothes. Challenges, or opportunities, come our way every single day. Some opportunities we take, some we let go, and some we ought to avoid. Some opportunities are temptations that we know are going to result in pain, tragedy, or heartbreak, and we need to let them pass us by. But some opportunities should be seized—opportunities that don't come around every day, opportunities that should be grabbed.

Have you met any of those opportunities lately? Did they walk up to you and invite you to come along? Did you seize them or did you let them pass by?

Jesus writes a letter to the church in Philadelphia beginning in Rev. 3:7. Opportunity is embedded in this letter. It has *challenge* scrolled all through it. This letter is like one of those strange pictures people stand and stare at to see an image appear within the pattern. The first time I saw someone looking at one of those pictures I thought, *That guy is caught like a deer in the headlights. Why would someone just stand and stare at a picture like that?* Then I began to look at it, and suddenly I said, "Oh, yeah! I see it. Yeah, I see it." It was like entering a new world.

If you study this letter, you'll eventually think, *Oh, yeah! There it is. I see the challenge!* This letter is just filled with challenge; it's full of opportunity.

To the angel of the church in Philadelphia, write:

These are the words of him who is holy and true, who holds the key of David. What he opens no one can shut, and what he shuts no one can open. I know your deeds. See, I have placed before you an open door that no one can shut. I know that you have little strength, yet you have kept my word and have not denied my name. I will make those who are of the synagogue of Satan, who claim to be Jews though they are not, but are liars—I will make them come and fall down at your feet and acknowledge that I have loved you. Since you have kept my command to endure patiently, I will also keep you from the hour of trial that is going to come upon the whole world to test those who live on the earth.

I am coming soon. Hold on to what you have, so that no one will take your crown. Him who overcomes I will make a pillar in the temple of my God. Never again will he leave it. I will write on him the name of my God and the name of the city of my God, the new Jerusalem, which is coming down out of heaven from my God; and I will also write on him my new name. He who has an ear, let him hear what the Spirit says to the churches. (Vv. 7-13)

For us to really see and understand the challenge in this letter, we need to know a little about the city of Philadelphia, so I invite you to walk with me through the gates of that city.

Philadelphia was the youngest of all the cities mentioned in Revelation. It was located in an area known for its agricultural products but also for earthquakes. Several times in this young city's life it was destroyed, either partially or totally, by earthquakes. The latest one had happened in AD 37, a few years before the writing of this letter, so most people lived in fear of the earthquakes. Most of them didn't live in the city proper, or within the city limits of Philadelphia. They lived more on the outskirts where they would not be as likely to have buildings falling on them.

Philadelphia was named for the king of Pergamos (or Pergamum) and was settled by the people from Pergamos. We looked at the church in that city in chapter 4. The king of Pergamos was named Attalas, and his nickname was Philadelphos. He was called Philadelphos (which means "one who loves his brother") because of his great affection for his brother. In that day, it was not uncommon for the man who was king to kill all of his brothers and anyone else who would threaten his throne. But Attalas was different, for he loved and cared for his brother and brought him into the fold.

Philadelphia was about a day's walk from the city of Sardis, which we examined in chapter 6, but it was miles from Sardis in its nature. In the letter to Sardis, for example, the church was rebuked without being given a commendation first. Jesus went right to the problem, and he commended them after the rebuke. In the letter to the church of Philadelphia, Jesus highly commends the church. In fact, the churches of Smyrna and Philadelphia were the only two churches that did not receive a rebuke from Jesus. There is no internal problem that Jesus addresses.

Philadelphia was known for two things. First, it was established by the king of Pergamos to be a military city to protect Pergamos. Thus it had many soldiers in and around it.

Second, the city was established to be a missionary city of Greek culture. It was born in Greek culture—Greek philosophy, thought, architecture, and way of life. If you wanted to know how

Greeks lived and what a Greek civilization was like, you could go to the city of Philadelphia and experience everything Greek. People would come in, absorb the Greek thought and practices, and then take that culture to their hometowns.

Jesus, then, gets right to his commendation and praise of the church. He first commends the people for their good works. They were giving of themselves to advance the cause of Christ. They were ministering well, and the Father was receiving the glory.

A church cannot accomplish anything good or lasting without God. We're to do good works in his name and let people see them and glorify God in heaven. We can do nothing without God but fail, so we are to give him the glory when we succeed. When God invites us to partner with him and we only do "what is expected of us," God in his grace, mercy, and love comes along with us. He not only equips us and enables us to do these things but also commends us for doing them. That's just the grace of God.

Jesus commended them not only for good works but also for their obedience to the Word. In that day, the Word for them would have been the Old Testament. And he was saying to them, "This is a Greek city, and you are following the Word, the Old Testament."

Do you remember the central message, the primary commandment, of the Old Testament? Jesus summarized it when He said to love God with all your heart, soul, strength, and mind, and to "love your neighbor as yourself" (see Luke 10:27). He says that is the sum of all the law, all the prophets, all the writings—love God with all your heart, soul, mind, and strength, and love your neighbor as you love yourself. And this church was keeping the Word. This church was *doing* the Word. These people loved God with everything in them, and they loved their neighbors as they loved themselves.

Jesus added perseverance to the list of commendations. He said, "In the face of trial and trouble and struggle, you have persevered" (see Rev. 3:8, 10). This church was much like the church in Smyrna; they had been excluded from the society because they refused to worship at the temples in the city or engage in the immorality of the local culture. As a result they lost jobs and businesses. They were living in difficult days, yet they persevered and Jesus called that commendable. What really matters is not our influence over humanity but our faithfulness before God. Jesus commends this church and, again, does not bring up a problem.

This letter is not about a crisis in the church. Unlike most of the other letters, this letter is about a *challenge*. This letter is about an opportunity for ministry. Now notice what Jesus says in verse 8: "I know your deeds [your good works, those things you're doing]. See, I have placed before you an open door that no one can shut."

Some doors are locked. Some open doors lead to places we don't need to go. Not every open door is a door Jesus has opened. But he does hold some doors open for us. And here is a church to whom Jesus is saying, "I have opened a door for you."

What does Jesus mean by that? Well, Paul uses that phrase in 1 Corinthians when he says, "A great door for effective work has opened to me, and there are many who oppose me" (16:9). In 2 Cor. 2:12, Paul used the phrase, "Now when I went to Troas to preach the gospel of Christ and found that *the Lord had opened a door for me*" (emphasis added). In Col. 4:3, he wrote, "And pray for us, too, that God may *open a door* for our message, so that we may proclaim the mystery of Christ, for which I am in chains" (emphasis added). So this concept of an open door is the idea of a challenge or an opportunity.

Jesus is writing to the church and says, "I have opened a door before you. I'm standing there holding this door wide open for you" (see v. 8). So what would have kept people from walking through that open door?

There were several hindrances. We find the first right here in the scripture—they had very little strength. He said, "I know your strength, your *little* strength'" (see v. 8). The Greek words used are actually *micros* and *dunamis*, or the words for "little" and "power." In other words, "You have micropower."

Have you ever felt as though you had micropower? You work all day, you're worn out, you come home, you put your feet up—you have micropower. It is spent after a full day's work. And then you realize you've got another day's work to do at home, yet all you have left is micropower.

Jesus tells this church, "You have very little power." Now this may have referred to the size of the congregation; it may have referred to the church's influence. We're not sure. But even though the people were weak, they were working. They were doing what they could with what they had. They didn't use their micropower as an excuse to do nothing. Instead, they did what they could with what they had.

We are all aware of our weaknesses in our churches. We don't have a lot of power. You may actually attend a large church with many people in your congregation. But when you compare your church to the mission before you, you'd have to admit that you have micropower, very little power. And we don't have a lot of buying power. I'm still waiting for someone to come forward and say, "Pastor, here's a check for five million dollars. Go ahead and complete all the building projects you need." It just hasn't happened—yet.

So what do we do? Do we sit back and say, "Because we can't do it all, we will do nothing," or do we go ahead and do what we can with what we have? It's not *how much* we do that matters most, but it's what we do with what we have that counts. And so I can identify with this church in Philadelphia—very little strength.

Their second hindrance was opposition from other people. If you read between the lines of this letter, you find there was a group of people who opposed this church. But in the same manner as the church in Smyrna, this church did not quit.

Let's be honest. Both as a church, corporately, and as individuals, we all have faced and will face opposition in our lives. Clearly we have an enemy who wants to see us defeated. We have an enemy who wants to see every single person in bondage or back in bondage. We have an enemy who wants to see us fail—again. We have an enemy who wants to keep us from walking through the doors Jesus is holding open for us.

To use the military metaphor associated with this city, if we're going to pull down strongholds, if we're going to assault the very gates of hell, if we are going to be a place where the enemy is defeated, we are going to have to face an enemy who doesn't want to see us succeed, an enemy who wants to bind us and take away our freedom. We have an enemy. And that enemy is going to do everything in his power to keep us from accomplishing the mission God has called us to achieve. You can count on it. It's going to happen. We're going to face that enemy as a church and as individuals. Whether we have battled with addictions in the past, made mistakes, or just lived peaceful lives, whatever our lives may be, there is an enemy of our souls who wants to defeat us.

But notice the church in Philadelphia did not let that stop them. They did not lose their sense of mission. They did not walk away from the challenge.

The door was open for them, and the door is open for us. We have a mission to build a bridge between Christ and our culture, to build a bridge between his power and the needs of people, to build a bridge between his kingdom and our world. Our mission comes from God.

We have an opportunity.

In my mind's eye, I see Jesus holding a door open for us. Where does that doorway lead? Look around your church and its neighborhood. Are there people needing help with recovery from drug abuse? Are neighboring schools desperate for support for their students and families? Do you find single parents looking for help in rebuilding their families following painful divorces? Do you see people who have everything they want materially and yet are bankrupt emotionally and spiritually? What are the specific and genuine needs in the community surrounding your church? Jesus is standing there holding a door wide open for you. Will you walk through it?

In your workplace, Jesus is holding a door open for you. People around you are battling illness, trying to make sense out of life. People you know are going through divorce, trying to figure it all out. People you work with are struggling with kids who seem to have lost their minds. So what do you do? Jesus is holding a door wide open for you.

We have opposition and hindrances. For example, one of the main needs in churches is simply human resources. We need

- teachers to teach discipleship classes, Bible studies, and recovery groups
- musicians for choirs and orchestras
- greeters to welcome people as they enter
- folks to support our churches in prayer
- caregivers to call on elderly people
- mentors for youth, children, and adults
- people to invest themselves in the lives of newly married couples
- people to tithe regularly and give generously

There are always hindrances to ministry. The enemy is going to try to defeat us. But notice who wrote the letter:

These are the words of him who is holy [that is, with spiritual authority and power] and true [meaning, with integrity, authenticity, relational authority, and power], who holds the key of David [the key to the kingdom, the key that says who gets in and who gets out, which doors are opened and which doors are closed. He has that positional authority and power. And then he says,] What he opens no one can shut. (V. 7)

You may be thinking, *Yeah, but I don't have any strength.* That's all right; it's not going to cause the door to be shut. *But I have micropower.* That's okay; the door's not going to be shut. *Yeah, but I've got all these issues that are hindering me.* That's okay; the door's still open—because *he's* holding the door open; *he* has the keys. No one can come in and take the keys. He's holding the door wide open for you. No one is going to close it.

So what do we do?

He tells us, "Hold on" (v. 11).

He's not talking about a survival mentality. Some Christians over the years have heard that phrase, "Hold on," and they think it means, "Don't change." That's not what it means. It's not about a survival mentality, as if you're sailing through a storm and you reach over and grab the center mast and just hang on for dear life, trying to ride out the storm. That's not what this word means. The word means "seize"—"seize the opportunity." It doesn't mean sitting back and saying, "Lord, help us just get through this life." No! It means walking through the door Jesus has opened and seizing the opportunity he has placed before us.

My mom trained me to hold the door open for people, especially for ladies. At times I've stood holding the door open for a person I thought was entering but who never did. Have you ever done that? If so, what did you do? Stand there forever? Of course not. After a few moments when you saw the person wasn't going to enter, you let the door close.

I wonder how many times Christ has walked up and held the door open for a church, but the church refused to walk through. How many times has Christ said, "Okay, since this church is refusing, I'll go open the door for another church."

In the kingdom of God, when we walk through one open door, it leads us to other open doors. We keep walking from one open door to another, because Jesus keeps holding doors open for those who are willing to walk through them.

As this letter draws to a close, Jesus gives us hope—the promise of victory for those "who overcome" (v. 12). Notice that a hope is different from a wish. I wish I had a billion dollars. There's no hope of that happening. Hope, however, is based on possibility. Jesus has given us possibility. And his promise is even stronger than possibility—it is assurance. He says in verse 12, "Him who overcomes I will make a pillar in the temple of my God."

Do you remember what Jesus identified earlier as the weakness of the church in Philadelphia? It possessed little strength—micropower. But what does a pillar in the temple represent? It's a symbol of strength—megapower, because pillars support the temple; they hold it up. Jesus is telling the church, "You who have micropower are going to become a picture of megapower."

How? By your own power? No, by *his* power. He says, "*I* will make" (v. 12, emphasis added). You may say, "We can't do it. We don't have the power; we don't have the funds or the resources. We don't have the people." But Jesus says, "Those issues are irrelevant. The door is open. Walk through it. I will make you strong. I will supply what you need."

You've probably heard the phrase "carpe diem." It's an ancient Latin phrase that means "seize the day." That is, "Make the most of the opportunity before you, walk through the open door—grab hold of the rope, swing out, and go into that backward dive as though there's nothing left to lose."

"He who has an ear, let him hear what the Spirit is whispering in his ear" (see v. 13).

As you contemplate your church and your life, what challenge is the Holy Spirit whispering to you? What is Jesus showing you and saying, "Here is your chance, your opportunity. Here's where your life can be empowered and used by me to make the world around you different. Here it is. Seize the day."

Take hold of *it*. Don't let anyone rob you of this opportunity. Don't listen to the enemy as he tells you that you're too weak or too small, that you don't have enough resources, or that the task is too big. Instead, listen to the Spirit whisper in your ear, "Carpe diem—seize the day." Jesus is holding the door for you.

"These are the words of him who is holy and true, who holds the key of David. . . . He who has an ear, let him hear what the Spirit says to the churches" (vv. 7, 13). And what is he saying?

"There is an open door of opportunity for you—carpe diem."

Questions for Discussion and Reflection

1. This chapter opens with a story about challenges—or as some call them, opportunities. "Some opportunities we take, some we let go, and some we ought to avoid" (p. 104). What kind of challenges, or opportunities, have you met lately?

2. Jesus commends the church in Philadelphia for their deeds—their good works. If Jesus was writing a letter to your church, what "good works" would he mention?

3. Philadelphia was a center for Greek culture. Jesus also commends the church's obedience to the Word. The author points out that the church was *doing* the Word in a culture that was anti-Christian, anti-Christ. Sound familiar? Discuss the challenges of *doing* the Word in an anti-Christian culture.

4. "Jesus is writing to the church and says, 'I have opened a door before you. I'm standing there holding this door wide open for you.' . . . So what would have kept people from walking through that open door?" (see p. 109). What keeps us from walking through the doors that Jesus holds open for us?

5. This chapter refers to "micropower" (see p. 109). Discuss the meaning of this term and its implications for us as individuals and as churches.

6. Another hindrance discussed in this chapter was "opposition from other people. If you read between the lines of this letter, you find there was a group of people who opposed this church" (p. 110). Is this still true today? What should our response be? What are some other hindrances that face our churches/ministries today?

7. Despite hindrances, we have a challenge before us—an opportunity—a door held open by Jesus himself. What doors are being held open in your life? In the life of your church?

8
KNOCK-
KNOCK

Our kids would always come home from their first day of school with knock-knock jokes. What was especially funny about their knock-knock jokes was that the kids thought the jokes were new.

Do you remember the first time you heard a knock-knock joke? No? Me neither. We all just grew up knowing knock-knock jokes. When I went to college and started dating my future wife, Karan, she taught me a new knock-knock joke:

"Knock-knock."

"Who's there?"

"Butch, Jimmy, and Al."

"Butch, Jimmy, and Al who?"

"Butch your arms around me, Jimmy a little kiss, and Al be happy."

That was a pretty good joke. And it worked! As I write this chapter, we are celebrating our twenty-seventh anniversary.

Beginning in Rev. 3:14, Jesus writes a letter to the church in Laodicea. In this letter is depicted an image of Jesus standing at the door and knocking, but this is no joke. This image is serious.

To the angel of the church in Laodicea write:

These are the words of the Amen, the faithful and true witness, the ruler of God's creation. I know your deeds, that you are neither cold nor hot. I wish you were either one or the other! So, because you are lukewarm—neither hot nor cold—I am about to spit you out of my mouth. You say, "I am rich; I have acquired wealth and do not need a thing." But you do not realize that you are wretched, pitiful, poor, blind and naked. I counsel you to buy from me gold refined in the fire, so you can become rich; and white clothes to wear, so you can cover your shameful nakedness; and salve to put on your eyes, so you see.

Those whom I love I rebuke and discipline. So be earnest, and repent. Here I am! I stand at the door and knock.

If anyone hears my voice and opens the door, I will go in and eat with him, and he with me.

To him who overcomes, I will give the right to sit with me on my throne, just as I overcame and sat down with my Father on his throne.

He who has an ear, let him hear what the Spirit says to the churches. (Vv. 14-22)

For us to really understand what Jesus was saying to the church in Laodicea—and saying to us today—we need to know some of the background of the city of Laodicea.

Laodicea was located about six miles from Colossae, to whom the letter of Colossians was written. It was founded in 250 BC by a king named Antiochus, and he named it after his wife, Laodice. The city was originally designed to be a fortress, but the water supply was six miles away, so it really wasn't well suited to serve as a fortress. So it became known for three characteristics.

First, Laodicea was known for its wealth. Laodicea was the center of banking for the entire region of Asia. The people were so wealthy they constructed many expensive, large homes, the ruins of which can be seen even today. In AD 60, the city was almost destroyed by an earthquake, but the citizens were so wealthy they refused to accept funds from Rome for rebuilding.

Second, Laodicea was also known for its commercial life. It had a productive clothing industry. The Laodiceans raised a breed of sheep that was uniquely black and produced dark, silky, sleek wool. They wove this wool into expensive fabrics, and the clothing made from this wool made the Laodiceans extremely wealthy. They were very productive and were known for what you might call their designer clothes.

Finally, Laodicea was known as a medical city; it was acclaimed for its medical knowledge. The Laodiceans produced a remarkable kind of ear-and-eye salve. Students would come to the city for medical training and would purchase this salve. You're probably familiar with the symbol often used for medicine—a caduceus (a staff with two serpents intertwined). It is believed by historians that the caduceus was the emblem of Laodicea. There was a medical cult in the city, the cult of Asclepius, which used the caduceus as its symbol. Here we are, over two thousand years later, still familiar with that symbol.

So you might say Laodicea was a Bank of America, a Nordstrom, and a Mayo Clinic all rolled into one. It was a city of culture.

As in all of his letters, Jesus identifies himself at the beginning and includes in his self-identification something that he will be addressing in the body of the letter. For example, he says, "I am the Amen" (see v. 14). The word "amen" points to a significant truth. In the gospel of John, you will find these words, especially in the King James Version: "Verily, verily I say unto you . . ." Jesus uses this phrase to emphasize the truth of what he's about to say. In the *New International Version*, that phrase is translated, "I tell you the truth . . ." But in the original Greek text, the phrase is actually two words: "Amen, amen." That is, "Pay attention; I am about to tell you something very significant."

The word "amen" also indicates the last or final word. For example, when we get to the end of a prayer, we always say, "Amen." Jesus says he is the Amen, the Last Word.

For Jesus to say he is the Last Word means

- cancer does not have the last word
- the doctor does not have the last word
- the boss at work does not have the last word
- discouraging circumstances do not have the last word
- fate does not have the last word

Jesus has the last word—he is the Amen, and what he says is significant, true, and will happen. He's the Amen.

Jesus then identifies himself as "the faithful and true witness" (v. 14). A witness is someone who has seen something. Jesus has credibility. He knows what he's talking about. He has observed what is happening among the Laodicean Christians, in their world, in their lives—and in our lives—so he bears witness to what he has seen, and he speaks the truth.

Jesus also identifies himself as "the ruler of God's creation" (v. 14). The word "ruler" here actually means source. He is the *source* of all creation. In this introductory phrase Jesus is establishing his authority to make these statements about the church. He's saying, "I gave the church life, so I have a right to speak to the church." The same is true of us. Jesus has given us life, so he has the right to speak to us about the condition of that life.

With all this in mind, we can begin to look at this letter in more detail and greater understanding.

As in all of his letters, Jesus expresses his knowledge of the church: "[I know you,] I know your deeds" (v. 15). But unlike all of his other letters, he has no commendation. In all of the other letters, Jesus commends the church for something, however small the positive trait may be. Somewhere in the other letters, he says, "Well, at least you're doing this," or "You're doing this one thing well," or "You have a few people who get it." But in this letter, there is no commendation, no praise, no approval. The church in Laodicea has the infamous distinction of being the only church about which Jesus had nothing good to say. Instead, he gets straight to the problem.

You've probably heard sermons or read lessons on this passage of Scripture that identify the church's problem as its level of commitment. You've possibly heard people interpret Jesus saying in this passage, "I wish you were either [hot or cold]" (v. 15), as if "hot" means committed and "cold" means really not committed; that Jesus is just saying, "So either be for me or against me; make up your mind." But do you think Jesus would ever want us to be against him? Of course not. Jesus wants us to be on his side. He wants us to be committed to him. He's not satisfied with lukewarm. He's not satisfied with a halfhearted commitment. And he's certainly not pleased with us being against him. So the problem he's addressing here is something that lies far deeper.

You might read this letter and recognize that the people of Laodicea had a problem with their self-image.

- They thought they were rich, but they were really poor.
- They thought they could see, but they were really blind.
- They thought they could hear, but they were really deaf.
- They thought they were well dressed, but they were shamefully naked.

The church in Laodicea suffered from identity blindness. They did not see themselves as God saw them. Their self-image was so inflated, they couldn't see it clearly. In verse 17, Jesus says, "But you do not realize . . ." The word "realize" literally means "see." He says, "You can't even see it—you don't see who you really are."

Sometimes we suffer from identity blindness because our egos are so inflated and we think we are rich; we think we own the world, and we just let everybody else walk around in it. At other times our identity blindness manifests itself in our inability to see ourselves as valuable, as objects of God's love, as objects of God's grace. In the case of the Laodiceans the problem was the first flaw—they had an inflated view of themselves. They couldn't see themselves as God really saw them. In this letter Jesus says, "You say you are rich, but who you are is much different" (see v. 17). In other words, "Here's what you say, but here's what you are."

So one of the issues Jesus is addressing is identity blindness. And it's true; we need to see ourselves as God sees us. But that is still not the main emphasis of this letter. That's still not the heart of the problem Jesus is addressing here. It lies deeper still.

Look at the temperature of the water, "neither hot nor cold" (v. 16). The word "hot," as used here, means "boiling point," or "hot to the point of boiling."

Our church softball team played in the city tournament recently. We're basically a middle-aged team. As I was playing third base, I looked around at my teammates and realized that we're all getting up there in age. We came in fourth this year, and we won the tournament last year, but let me tell you, after the third game of this year's tournament, my body was sore. Don't tell my teammates, but I was so sore I didn't mind losing. After the game I went home and took a hot bath. Soaking sore muscles in that hot water is good for healing. It loosens up old, sore muscles.

About six miles away from the city of Laodicea was an area with hot springs. People would come from miles around to sit in these hot springs because it was good for healing. So when Jesus said, "I wish you were [hot]" (v. 15), immediately in their minds they saw those hot springs and thought, *Yeah, I know what you're talking about.*

Then when Jesus said, "I wish you were [cold]" (v. 15), that word "cold" means "cold to the point of freezing."

Have you ever been to Sliding Rock, North Carolina? It is a slab of rock over which runs a mountain stream that collects in a natural pool at the bottom before continuing its trek down the mountain. I love that place! I was a kid the last time I went, but we had so much fun sliding down that rock into the pool of water at the bottom. The sliding expanse of rock was about forty feet long, and the water temperature in August is about thirty-two to thirty-three degrees Fahrenheit. If the water was not flowing, it would likely be frozen solid. Usually you can jump into cold water and get used to it. You never get used to this water. We would slide down the rock to the bottom and scream because we knew that icy water was waiting for us. We would then climb from the freezing, cold water feeling totally refreshed.

Similarly, on a really hot day, when you're dry and thirsty, you don't want lukewarm water. You want ice-cold water.

About six miles away from Laodicea in a different direction from the hot springs were some ice-cold springs, artesian springs, that bubbled up cold, refreshing water.

So when Jesus said, "I wish you were hot [good for healing] or cold [good for refreshing]," the people knew exactly what he was referring to.

Notice that Jesus pronounces the Laodiceans lukewarm, neither hot nor cold. They were, in essence, good for nothing. Jesus looks at this church and says, "You think you're rich, that you're all dressed up, that you can see, that you can hear; but you're pitiful, poor, blind, and naked. You're wretched. Good for nothing" (see v. 17).

What is the problem here? If Laodiceans are lukewarm, they're not good for healing or refreshing. So what had made them lukewarm?

Part of the problem was that they were not fulfilling their mission. They forgot what they were supposed to do, who they were supposed to be.

Jesus never intended the church to be a country club. Jesus certainly wants us to live in fellowship with one another. Jesus wants us to walk together as a community. He wants us to enjoy one another on the journey of life. Perhaps we've experienced difficulties, and looking back on them, we thank God that we had the support of our brothers and sisters in Christ—that they prayed for us and helped us get through those difficult times. We are to carry one another's burdens (see Gal. 6:2). That is part of the mission of the church. But we are never to be an exclusive country club that exists only for the benefit of its members.

Jesus never intended the church to be a performing arts center. We're not an entertainment center. We thank God for people with musical talents, but we don't have choirs and orchestras for the purpose of entertainment. Their purpose is to lead us in worship. Only Jesus Christ is worthy of all praise. Only he is to be worshipped. Everything musicians do in a church service is designed to bring honor and glory to him. It's not about entertainment.

The church is not even a political action group. We should be involved in our culture and used by Jesus to transform our world. We must be active against the injustices of our society. But Jesus never intended the church to exist simply to make political change. Our hope is not in the Republican Party, the Democratic Party, a third party, or any political party. "[Our] hope is built on nothing less," as the old hymn says, "than Jesus' blood and righteousness."[7] That is the only foundation for our hope. We're to be involved in our culture and help bring about positive change, but that is not the main mission of our existence.

The hot and cold issue is symptomatic of the real problem. Verse 19 says, "Those whom I love I rebuke and discipline. So be earnest, and repent. Here I am! I stand at the door and knock. If anyone hears my voice and opens the door, I will come in and eat with him, and he with me." You've probably seen the pictures of Jesus standing at a dimly lit wooden door, knocking to come in. So where is he in all of these pictures? He is on the outside of the door trying to get inside.

The *real* problem here is that the church of Laodicea had excluded or locked Jesus out. Can you imagine that? He's writing to his church and saying, "Let me in. Why have you shut me out?" Most of the time this verse is applied only to individuals, but that's only secondary; it first applies to the church. Jesus wrote this letter to a church that was strategically positioned to make the world different. Yet this church was basically good for nothing; they had excluded Jesus. They had kicked him out of his own church and locked the door. So here is Jesus saying, "Please, just let me in."

Too many churches today operate without Jesus. They have positioned themselves financially so that there is no faith involved in expanding ministry. They only do what they can do by their own resources. They don't need Jesus. So they lock him out. They don't walk in obedience when Jesus leads them in a new direction, because they may upset people—as if they needed the resources of people more than Jesus himself.

As I've been writing these words, I've been praying for the church I pastor and asking, "O God, please do not ever let us lock you out of this church—this community of faith. O God, never let us get to the place where we think we can do even one positive thing apart from you. Never let us get to the place where we believe we can do anything of importance by our own will, our own accord, or our own ability. O God, keep us Christ centered. Keep us focused on you so that you are the focal point of all our gatherings and of all our life. Never let us become complacent with our accomplishments. Keep us dependent on you and obedient when you want to do a new thing through us. Whatever we do, Lord, it must be all about you."

Now let's apply this to our lives as individuals. Are there any areas of your life where you have excluded Jesus, locked him out of your life? You may be thinking, *Of course not, Dwight. I*

haven't locked Jesus out of my life. I'm a believer. I'm a Christian.
Okay, so you gave him the laundry room with all the filth and
said, "Thank you, Jesus, for forgiving me of my sins and clean-
ing up my life." Well, what about that room of bitterness? What
about that room where the attitudes are kept locked away. Don't
you just hate it when someone opens that door and the attitudes
fall off the shelf, making a mess of things? What about the room
where the habits hide, you know, the ones we try to justify? Is he
standing outside of those doors, asking, "Why don't you let me
in? Here I am. I'm standing at the door and knocking."

That's the problem most Christians live with. We want Jesus to be Lord of our lives and free us from sin, but we don't
want him to be Lord of our lives *totally*, completely, and without
any reservation. We don't say, "Jesus, come in. Make yourself at
home. You have the key. It's all yours."

When we let Jesus be Master of the house, it is no longer our
house; it becomes *his* house. It's not your temple anymore; it's *his*
temple. Is it your life? Not anymore; it's *his* life. And he wants to
live it through you. That means you have to give him control of
all those areas of your life. Everything! Without fail! No holding
anything back! "Lord, here it is. It's all yours."

Now don't miss the warning. Jesus loves us so much that he
gives us a word of caution. He says, "'Here I am! I stand at the
door and knock.' If you don't open the door, I will 'spit you out of
my mouth'" (see vv. 16, 20). The word literally means "vomit"
out of his mouth.

Think about it. He's the "Amen" and "the faithful and true
witness," "the ruler of God's creation" (v. 14). In the gospel of
John (same author as Revelation), Jesus was referred to as the
spoken Word. The common idea here is speaking. The one who
speaks the "amen," the one who speaks as "the faithful and true
witness," the one who is the spoken Word of God, is going "to

spit you [vomit you] out of [his] mouth" (see vv. 14, 16); that is, he will reject you from the body of Christ. He's not going to live with this.

But you have a choice: "If anyone hears my voice and opens the door, I will come in and eat with him, and he with me" (v. 20). Jesus says he will supply everything we need. That's our hope. He said, "Take what you need from me."

Jesus was trying to get through to the Laodiceans, "You think you're rich. You think you've got all this great stuff. You think everything is good, but I'm advising you: 'Buy from me'" (see vv. 17-18). But he doesn't want us to pay a price for it. He simply wants us to come to him, because he is the source of everything we need, whether it's financial help, business advice, medical insight, spiritual wholeness, or clothing us with purity, as he says, "I will cover your shameful ways. I will put salve on your eyes 'so you can see'" (see v. 18). He'll make us whole. But we have to go to him.

Jesus loves us enough to challenge us: "Those whom I love I rebuke and discipline" (v. 19). It's tough love. Have you been rebuked lately? Has he challenged you lately? Jesus loves us enough to meet us where we are. "Here I am! I stand at the door" (v. 20). He's not calling to us from somewhere else. He's here, right here.

He says, "If anyone hears my voice and opens the door, I will come in and eat with him, and he with me" (v. 20).

Now I love this part. He talks about eating together, fellowship, but look how close this fellowship is. He says, "To him who overcomes, I will give the right to sit with me on my throne, just as I overcame and sat down with my Father on his throne" (v. 21). Do you see the relationship between the Father and the Son? He says that the same relationship, the same intimacy, the same closeness, is there for you. So no matter what you're going through, no matter what the situation is, no matter what's behind door number one, door number two, door number three, or all those other rooms we want to lock God out of—no matter what, he says, "If you'll just open those doors, I'll come in. We'll fellowship together, and when we fellowship together, I will do in you what needs to be done."

So what was the problem with the church in Laodicea? The problem with the church is the same problem in many churches today. It is the same problem in the lives of many believers today. Jesus is locked out.

Have you locked Jesus out of any area of your life? He says, "He who has an ear, let him hear what the Spirit says to the churches" (v. 22).

Is there some area of your life about which the Holy Spirit is asking, "Why have you locked me out of this room? Is this is an area you don't want me to enter?"

Pray about that area of your life. Open the door and allow Jesus to be Master of every part your life.

And if you hear "knock-knock," don't hesitate to answer, "Who's there." And if you hear the voice of Jesus, please let him in.

Questions for Discussion and Reflection

1. What issues/circumstances in our lives try to have the *last word*? Who really has the last word?

2. Over the years teachers of this letter have often interpreted the hot and cold imagery as being for or against Christ. What is the problem with this interpretation? (see pp. 124-26).

3. How has the church struggled with its identity? In what ways have Christians struggled with identity?

4. How can the church be a healing agent today?

5. How can the church be a refreshing agent today?

6. How has the image of Jesus standing at the door, knocking, been used in the past?

7. In what ways has the church locked Jesus out? Are there any areas of your life where you have excluded Jesus, locked him out?

8. The author writes: "Jesus loves us enough to challenge us: 'Those whom I love I rebuke and discipline.' . . . It's tough love. Have you been rebuked lately? Has [Jesus] challenged you lately?" (p. 129). Is your life open to the knocking, challenging, rebuking presence of Christ?

9. The challenges Jesus issues to our lives flow from his love for us. The changes he makes surface in our fellowship (eating) with him. How can we improve our fellowship with Jesus, thereby giving him full permission to challenge and change us?

9
ONE MORE
LETTER

God is love. Everything he does, everything he says, everything he is—*everything* reflects his supreme essence. God is love in its purest, holiest, and most eternal sense.

When we embrace that view of God, the choices he makes for us, and the messages he sends to us, we are able to read the letters Jesus writes to the New Testament churches with clarity, understanding, and perspective. Everything he communicated to those churches came from a heart brimming with divine love. Some of the churches were floundering; Jesus directed them to the lighthouse to bring them back on course. Some of the churches had grasped the true ministry of Jesus Christ and embodied it as their own; Jesus commended them and encouraged them to stay the course and keep impacting their world with God's message of hope. Wherever each church was in its journey, Jesus spoke directly to that part of the body, identifying himself as the one who could take that church to the next step and enable it to accomplish his mission for it.

So what about the church today? What about your church? How do these letters relate to us?

I've taken the liberty—creative license—to paraphrase these seven letters into one letter to the church of our day. The church of the twenty-first century has some challenges and problems, but nothing that wasn't an issue two thousand years ago for the first Christian churches. Jesus' response (as communicated through John) in Revelation addresses almost every problem we face in the church today.

That's the point of these letters from Revelation. They're not just written to a small group of Christians who were at the starting line of establishing the most radical and important religious movement of all time. They're written not only to the people of the first century but also to *every group of believers* that identifies itself as a church of the Lord Jesus Christ. If a church is experiencing a problem or a loss of direction, Jesus' response is to be found in the letters.

So if Jesus chose to send another letter to the present-day church, what would he say? Would he say anything different from the messages he sent back then? And what would he think of how far we have—or haven't—come since the first set of letters was written on the Isle of Patmos?

Perhaps Jesus might take his divine pen in hand and write something like this to us:

Dear Church,

I am Jesus Christ, the Son of God the Father almighty, maker of heaven and earth. I was from the beginning, and I will be until the end. I have defeated the power of evil, and I have triumphed over death. My Father is holy love. I am the expression of his holy love in this world. I see you, I know you by name, and I love you. I will never change. I am.

I know where you live. I know your circumstances and the temptations you face. I am aware of the evil that dwells in the world, and I am familiar with the sin that surrounds you. I know everything you are doing amid your struggles. And I know that while some of you are holding fast to my grace and provision, some of you have taken it upon yourselves to chart your own course.

Do not be mistaken—apart from me you can do nothing. If you move out ahead of my will or in a direction I have not chosen for you, you will fail miserably. All of your efforts to prosper without my empowerment will be for nothing, and I will not bless plans or programs that have not come from my divine will. If you do not demonstrate my love to all those around you, the opportunity to be light in a dark and dying world will be lost. I have called you to glorify my name and not your own.

I am your source of strength, your foundation, your direction, and your future. I am totally sufficient for your every need.

With my presence, power, and will, there is no mission you can't accomplish. I have called you to carry my love into the world by the presence and power of the Holy Spirit, and what I have chosen you to do I will equip you to complete. Whatever you need, I will provide.

Hold fast to my promises. I will never abandon or forsake you. I will be constantly at your side to guide and protect you. Whoever is faithful in following me will reap the reward of abundant and eternal life. I will write upon you the name of my Father. You will be my people and will dwell with me in the house of the Lord forever.

"He who has an ear, let him hear what the Spirit says to the churches" (Rev. 3:22).

NOTES

1. Leonard Sweet, *SoulTsunami: Sink or Swim in the New Millennium Culture* (Grand Rapids: Zondervan, 1999), 16.

2. Neil Cole, *Organic Church: Growing Faith Where Life Happens* (San Francisco: Josey-Bass, 2005), 45.

3. Quoted in ibid., xxi.

4. Fritz Rienecker and Cleon L. Rogers, *Linguistic Key to the Greek New Testament* (Grand Rapids: Zondervan, 1982).

5. *Encarta World English Dictionary*, s.v. "encourage," http://encarta.msn.com/encnet/features/dictionary/DictionaryResults.aspx?lextype=3&search=encourage (accessed April 21, 2011).

6. Rienecker and Rogers, *Linguistic Key to the Greek New Testament*.

7. Edward Mote, "The Solid Rock," ca. 1834, Cyber Hymnal, http://www.hymntime.com/tch/htm/m/y/h/myhopeis.htm.

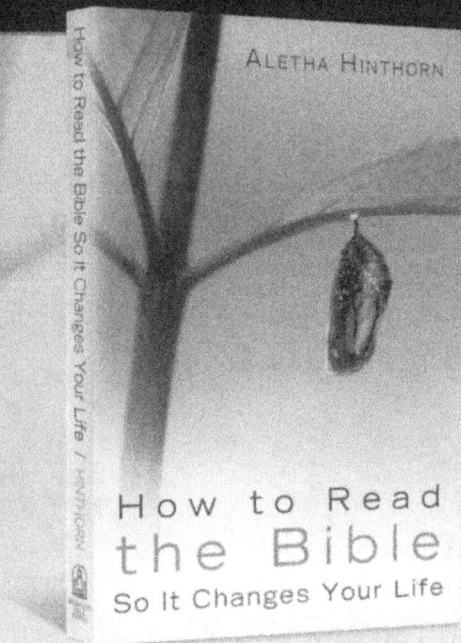

www.ingramcontent.com/pod-product-compliance
Lightning Source LLC
LaVergne TN
LVHW051414080426
835508LV00022B/3086

Advanced praise for Love vs. Fear

"*Love vs. Fear* is a beautiful and personal invitation to experience the extravagant love of our Heavenly Father and bask in His powerful protection and unfailing gentleness. Sylvia St.Cyr has captured the most important aspect of God's heart... His desire to walk alongside us as we trust Him to conquer the fears that hold us captive. Get ready to enjoy an engaging account of transparency and courageous self-reflection that will inspire you to receive everything you need to live your very best life! I highly recommend this book."

—Audrey Meisner, television host of *My New Day*
bestselling author of *Wake Up Smiling* and *Marriage Under Cover*

"*Love vs. Fear* is the beat of Sylvia's heart laid bare. Join her in a quest for true freedom from this world, for liberty with the One who knows it all."

—Amanda Legault, author of *In My Wake*

"Sylvia St.Cyr not only gets to the root of our deepest fears, but she gets to the deepest root of who we are. This book is filled with truth statements that are both accessible and profound—I find myself quoting it nonstop!"

—Matt Falk, comedian, writer, and actor,
placed second in the World Series of Comedy in Las Vegas

"Over the last two years, I have been forced to come face to face with my fears in a way that I hadn't before. Coming to terms with just how much my many fears tended to drive my attitude and actions has been a sobering and liberating realization. I've discovered in deep ways that perfect love is the only thing that can cast out fear. Knowing that I am loved unconditionally by God and that nothing I do or don't do can separate me from his love is something I have to revisit everyday. Thank you, Sylvia, for reminding me that "It is finished." I needed it."

—Tullian Tchividjian
bestselling author of *One-Way Love:*
Inexhaustible Grace for an Exhausted World

"In *Love vs. Fear*, Sylvia St.Cyr overcomes her fear and courageously unzips her heart to expose the love she has experienced firsthand. Through vulnerable self-disclosure, helpful professional insights, truth-infusing scripture, and personally applicable prayer, she reveals how fear can be flushed out and instead be replaced and transformed by the powerful and unconditional love of God. Thank you, Sylvia, for beautifully leading us to see how great the Father's love for us is and that perfect love, indeed, casts out all fear."

—Lisa Elliott
speaker and award-winning author of *The Ben Ripple*
and *Dancing in the Rain*

"*Love vs. Fear* is a great primer for those new to Christian faith and wondering how God's perfect love casts out all fear. Sylvia's personal experiences will encourage those who need a friend along the journey from fear to faith."

—Ellen Graf-Martin, blogger, speaker
and entrepreneur (www.ellengrafmartin.com)

"*Love vs. Fear* clarifies how significant a healthy identity is to facing fear. Sylvia leans heavy into her identity in God's eyes. She shares her most harrowing experience in life and how in that moment she felt acceptance rather than condemnation. As in my case, don't be surprised when you find yourself referring to something Sylvia wrote that proved to be just the right words to help love win over fear."

—Robert (Bob) Jones
pastor and author of *Ornament*

"As a gifted writer and communicator, it's been fun to watch Sylvia grab on to opportunities and not let fear get in her way. Sylvia's personal style of writing is honest and she is not afraid to delve into the messiness of life. If we can only grasp the simple truth in this book, of God's love and its power to embolden us with confidence, our lives will never be the same. I highly recommend *Love vs. Fear* for your personal library."

—Jeremy Braun
owner of Word Alive Press